James Brindley
Canal Engineer

A NEW PERSPECTIVE

with particular reference to his family background

Kathleen M Evans

with illustrations by the author

ACKNOWLEDGMENTS

This study was prompted by the discovery that a 17th century ancestress of mine, Ann Roe of Parwich, was a sister of James Brindley's great-grandmother, Alice Bowman. Thanks are due to friends and family, who made contributions in a variety of ways and to staff of the Science Museum, Kensington; of Glasgow City Archives, of British Waterways Archive, Gloucester Dock and the Religious Society of Friends, Bull Street, Birmingham.

In recent decades, amateur historians have drawn attention to documents containing further facts. Terry Baddeley, Tony Bonson, Gordon Brindley and Trevor Markin have researched different fields - a colliery, watermills, genealogy and pottery. I appreciate their willingness to share this new information.

Documents were produced at the following Record Offices and Libraries:
Staffordshire Record Office; Lichfield Record Office; William Salt Library, Stafford; Derbyshire Record Office; Cheshire Record Office; Nottinghamshire Record Office; Public Record Office; Birmingham Central Library; Stoke-on-Trent Central Library Archives; Derby Local Studies Library; Friends' House Library, Euston; Northumberland Record Office and the University of Keele Library (Archives Dept.).

Permission has been given for the reproduction of John Brindley's letter (23021-31) 'By Courtesy of the Trustees of the Wedgwood Museum, Barlaston, Stoke-on-Trent, Staffordshire, England' and Keele University Library, where the manuscript was deposited.
Permission has been given for the reproduction of James Brindley's letter (2DE/7/4/2) and William Brown's letter (2DE/6/3/1) by Northumberland Record Office.
Permission has been given for the reproduction of the signatures of James Brindley and Hugh Henshall and the view of the Stourport Basin (1802), by British Waterways Archive, Gloucester Dock.
Permission has been given for the reproduction of the will of James Brindley [senior], of Leek, probate 6 May 1773, by Lichfield Record Office.
Permission has been given for the reproduction of part of maps S 815 OS/SRM 14 Norton-in-the-Moors (1771) by Stoke-on-Trent Central Library Archives

ABBREVIATIONS

b	born	LRO	Lichfield Record Office
bap	baptised	m	married
BCL	Birmingham Central Library	N'land RO	Northumberland Record Office
bur	buried	NRO	Nottinghamshire Record Office
c	circa/about	PCC	Prerogative Court of Canterbury
CRO	Cheshire Record Office		(wills in PRO)
d	died	PRO	Public Record Office
DLSL	Derby Local Studies Library	SRO	Staffordshire Record Office
DRO	Derbyshire Record Office	WSL	William Salt Library, Stafford
SCLA	Stoke on Trent Central Library Archives		

CHURNET VALLEY BOOKS
1 King Street, Leek, Staffordshire. ST13 5NW 01538 399033

www.leekbooks.co.uk

© Kathleen Evans and Churnet Valley Books 2007
ISBN 978-1-904546 52 8

PREFACE

'...any circumstances of his life should be wrote down.'

Dr Erasmus Darwin (1772)

According to works of reference, James Brindley (1716-1772) was an engineering genius who worked on the foundation and construction of the British Canal system with dedication, his great ability enabling him to overcome many technical problems. Although the projects were promoted by influential people and discussed at length by committees, it was acknowledged that Brindley, the self-taught engineer, led the way as consultant. Brindley's work included ideas of lasting value and resulted in a total of over 360 miles of inland waterway. The importance of his contribution increased as the Industrial Revolution continued to evolve during the following century.

When Samuel Smiles wrote *Lives of the Engineers* (1862), he included a biography of Brindley as stories of success and rise to fame were popular in Victorian times. In 1841 RA Davenport's account of Brindley's life was entitled, *Lives of individuals who raise themselves from poverty to eminence and fortune*, so Smiles was not the first to write in this vein. Brindley's family was said to have been saddened by the stories of his humble background, but every family has its ups and downs in society and branches of descent can vary greatly through luck, educational opportunity, marriage and friendships, sending genealogical lines far apart in a few generations. Born in the hills of Derbyshire, Brindley lived and died in North Staffordshire, where people bearing the Brindley surname and especially those in the environs of Leek, are curious about his family. Brief character sketches of James Brindley, from scarce examples of his handwriting and a few legendary comments of associates, have left an air of mystery about the origins of one of the first to be called an 'engineer'.

Brindley's obituary notice was written by Thomas Bentley, using letters from his close friend Josiah Wedgwood, the potter. The work was expanded into a memoir appearing anonymously in the *Universal Magazine* (March 1780), eight years after Brindley's death and a mere six months after the demise of his mother in Leek. Hugh Henshall, Brindley's much younger brother-in-law, had supplied information - he had been Brindley's assistant surveyor for about ten years, but Wedgwood had known Brindley for double that period. Brothers-in-law do not always have accurate facts about their acquired relatives and although James Brindley's brother John was in business alongside the newly-built Trent and Mersey Canal, he had left home at the age of ten years and may not have been able to supply further information. Samuel Smiles's contribution became a popular narrative as he was able to produce a more detailed account of Brindley's constructions, but he was a journalist and eventually his approach was thought to contain a degree of exaggeration. Nevertheless, the detail is still to be valued.

A modern appreciation of Brindley's engineering can be found in two books published in 1968. Dr Cyril TG Boucher, the author of *James Brindley: Engineer 1716-1772*, restored the machinery of the derelict Brindley Mill at Leek for the Brindley Mill Preservation Trust prior to its opening as the Brindley Mill Museum in 1974. AG Banks and RB Schofield produced work on a different project, *Brindley at Wet Earth*

Colliery, An Engineering Study, for Brindley had constructed a weir and tunnelling at the Lancashire site.

The records of numerous canal committees require a completely different field of research from that undertaken here. The complex area of canal history has produced many books on waterways, incorporating details from minute books and visits to canals, tunnels and aqueducts. The present work has used a variety of documents not noted previously and should provide a greater knowledge of other aspects of Brindley's life. The research was initiated by the chance identification of his forebears and connections, and continued through original sources providing information on Brindley himself and the contemporary situation. Brindley's early notebook has been deciphered and his attendances at the Staffordshire and Worcestershire Canal construction are examined. Wedgwood's letters and the Boulton and Watt papers add a further glimpse into the period.

On hearing of the death of James Brindley, Dr Erasmus Darwin replied to his friend Josiah Wedgwood by letter, on 30 September 1772. The news '... *gave me sincere grief about Mr Brindley, whom I have always esteemed to be a great genius, and whose loss is truly a public one, I don't believe he has left his equal. I think the various Navigations should erect him a monument in Westminster Abbey, and hope you will at the proper time give them this hint'*, but no such steps were taken. Dr Darwin's letter also suggested that '... *any circumstances of his life should be wrote down'*.

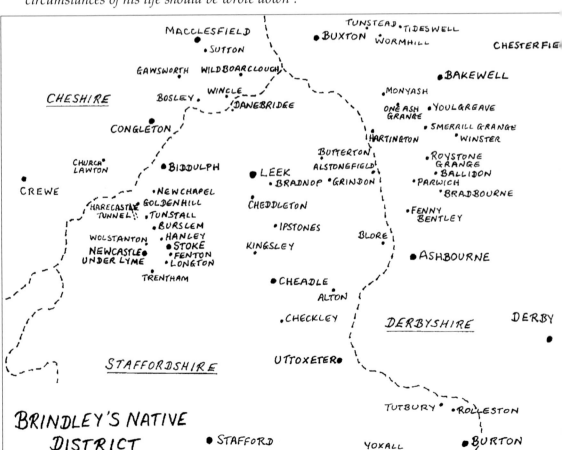

BRINDLEY'S NATIVE DISTRICT

Family Lines

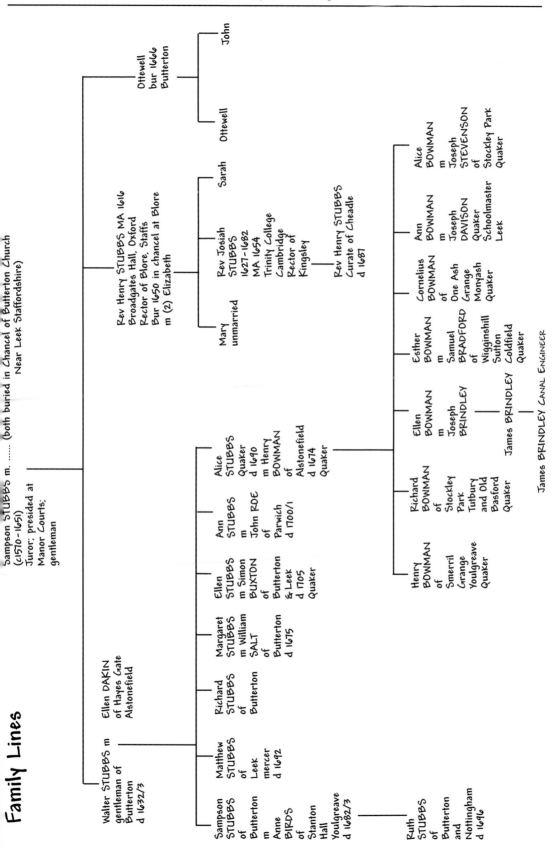

Sampson STUBBS m. ...... (both buried in Chancel of Butterton Church
Near Leek Staffordshire)
(c1570-1651)
Juror; presided at
Manor Courts;
gentleman

Walter STUBBS m   Ellen DAKIN
gentleman of   of Hayes Gate
Butterton   Alstonefield
d 1632/3

Rev Henry STUBBS MA 1616
Broadgates Hall, Oxford
Rector of Blore, Staffs
Bur 1650 in chancel at Blore
m (2) Elizabeth

Ottewell
bur 1606
Butterton

John

Ottewell

Sarah

Mary
unmarried

Rev Josiah
STUBBS
1627-1682
MA 1654
Trinity College
Cambridge
Rector of
Kingsley

Rev Henry STUBBS
Curate of Cheadle
d 1687

Matthew
STUBBS
of
Leek
mercer
d 1692

Richard
STUBBS
of
Butterton

Margaret
STUBBS
m William
SALT
of
Butterton
d 1675

Ellen
STUBBS
m Simon
BUXTON
of
Butterton
& Leek
d 1705
Quaker

Ann
STUBBS
m
John ROE
of
Parwich
d 1700/1

Alice
STUBBS
Quaker
d 1690
m Henry
BOWMAN
of
Alstonefield
d 1674
Quaker

Sampson
STUBBS
of
Butterton
m
Anne
BIRDS
of
Stanton
Hall
Youlgreave
d 1682/3

Ruth
STUBBS
of
Butterton
and
Nottingham
d 1696

Henry
BOWMAN
of
Smerril
Grange
Youlgreave
Quaker

Richard
BOWMAN
of
Stockley
Park
Tutbury
and Old
Basford
Quaker

Ellen
BOWMAN
m
Joseph
BRINDLEY

Esther
BOWMAN
m
Samuel
BRADFORD
of
Wigginshill
Sutton
Coldfield
Quaker

Cornelius
BOWMAN
of
One Ash
Grange
Monyash
Quaker

Ann
BOWMAN
m
Joseph
DAVISON
Quaker
Schoolmaster
Leek

Alice
BOWMAN
m
Joseph
STEVENSON
of
Stockley Park
Quaker

James BRINDLEY

James BRINDLEY CANAL ENGINEER

BRINDLEY

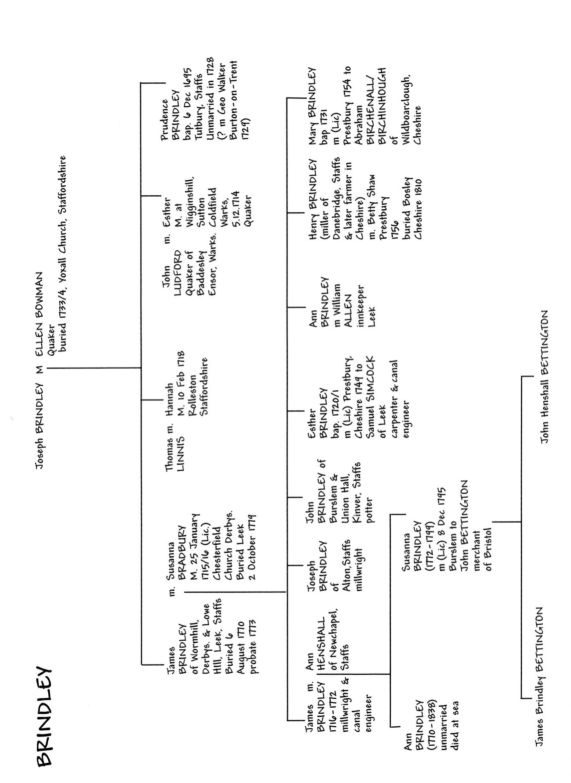

Joseph BRINDLEY M ELLEN BOWMAN
Quaker
buried 1733/4, Yoxall Church, Staffordshire

James BRINDLEY of Wormhill, Derbys. & Lowe Hill, Leek, Staffs Buried 6 August 1710 probate 1713 — m. Susanna BRADBURY M. 25 January 1715/16 (Lic.) Chesterfield Church Derbys. Buried Leek 2 October 1719

Thomas m. Hannah LINNIS M. 10 Feb 1718 Rolleston Staffordshire

John LUDFORD Quaker of Baddesley Ensor, Warks. m. Esther M. at Wigginshill, Sutton Coldfield Warks. 5.12.1714 Quaker

Prudence BRINDLEY bap. 6 Dec 1695 Tutbury, Staffs. Unmarried in 1728 (? m Geo Walker Burton-on-Trent 1729)

James m. Ann HENSHALL of Newchapel, Staffs BRINDLEY 1716-1772 millwright & canal engineer

Joseph BRINDLEY of Alton, Staffs millwright

John BRINDLEY of Burslem & Union Hall, Kinver, Staffs potter

Esther BRINDLEY bap. 1720/1 m (Lic) Prestbury, Cheshire 1749 to Samuel SIMCOCK of Leek carpenter & canal engineer

Ann BRINDLEY m William ALLEN innkeeper Leek

Henry BRINDLEY (miller of Danebridge, Staffs & later farmer in Cheshire) m. Betty Shaw Prestbury 1756 buried Bosley Cheshire 1810

Mary BRINDLEY bap 1731 m (Lic) Prestbury 1754 to Abraham BIRCHENALL/ BIRCHINHOUGH of Wildboarclough, Cheshire

Ann BRINDLEY (1770-1838) unmarried died at sea

Susanna BRINDLEY (1772-1799) m (Lic) 8 Dec 1795 Burslem to John BETTINGTON merchant of Bristol

John Henshall BETTINGTON

James Brindley BETTINGTON

BRINDLEY - HENSHALL - WILLIAMSON

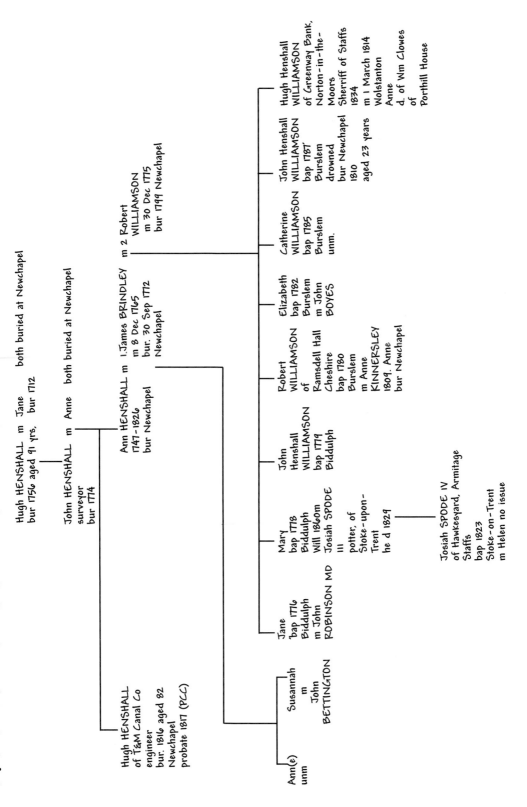

Memorial at Brindley's birthplace, Tunstead, Wormhill, Derbyshire

Brindley memorial at Wormhill

Smerrill Grange

CHAPTER 1
ROOTS

James Brindley was the eldest of the children born to James and Susanna on a holding at Tunstead, in the chapelry of Wormhill, part of the parish of Tideswell in Derbyshire. The ruins of the house are no longer visible, but the field where they stood was identified by an ash tree which grew through the old floor. A replacement tree flourishes by a short, plain column of stone bearing a plaque and the words:

JAMES BRINDLEY
1716-1772
MILLWRIGHT AND CIVIL ENGINEER
HERE STOOD THE COTTAGE IN WHICH JAMES BRINDLEY WAS BORN
OF HUMBLE BIRTH,
HE BECAME FAMOUS AS THE PIONEER BUILDER OF THE GREAT
CANALS OF ENGLAND.
THIS PLAQUE WAS ERECTED BY THE LOCAL HISTORY SECTION OF
THE DERBYSHIRE ARCHAEOLOGICAL SOCIETY AND UNVEILED BY
JL LONGLAND, ESQ. M.A. ON NOVEMBER 1 1958, WHEN MISS YHB
HARTFORD PLANTED THE ADJACENT ASH TREE.

This simple memorial stands close to the drystone wall bounding the narrow lane and farm below the ancient road between Wormhill and Buxton. At 1100 feet above sea level, it is a bleak spot on a dull day, being more exposed than the village itself and affording extensive views to Great Rocks Dale and beyond. One of the largest quarry faces in Europe has been developed in the Dale and its rim can be seen within half a mile of the Brindley memorial stone, although a partial screen of trees stands between the quarry and the present farm.

Brindley's Croft

In 1875, Wormhill erected a memorial to James Brindley in the form of a drinking fountain and trough surrounded by iron railings in a well-tended shrubbery. The Victorian-style monument of walls, steps and arches of stone is maintained with pride by the people of this sparsely-populated upland village.

Wormhill Church has been rebuilt since the time James Brindley may have been taken there for baptism, but only a single record of the Brindley family's residence in the parish appears in the register. Young James's sister, Esther Brindley, was christened in March 1720/1, although their father, also named James, had been brought up with his mother's Quaker relatives, whose creed did not include baptism. In addition, the curate of Wormhill, the Rev Robert Turnock, from Rudyard, near Leek, may have been ill for some time and unable to keep his register in order. Probate was granted on his brief will in 1721.

The roots of James Brindley senior were firmly in the moorland parishes of north Staffordshire, including Leek, but his family moved away and some of his early years were spent in the parish of Tutbury, in the east of the county. In 1687, his grandmother Alice Bowman (née Stubbs) established a Quaker Meeting house at Stockley Park, an ancient place at an entrance into the Needwood Forest. For decades, the large farmhouse with seven bedrooms housed several members of the Bowman family, but the last Bowman occupant was Alice Stevenson, the canal engineer's great-aunt. She left about the year 1730 after the death of her husband. Through Quakerism and Alice Bowman's management and bequests to her sons and daughters, the family was no longer confined to the moorlands.

Alice Bowman (c1630-1690) was a great-grandmother of James Brindley, the engineer, and a grand-daughter of Sampson Stubbs (c1565-1651) of Butterton, a small stony village above the Manifold valley. Sampson was a yeoman who became a local lawyer. From 1589, when he must have been at least twenty-one years of age, he was one of a panel of jurors at the Quarter Sessions in Stafford, firstly for the Duchy of Lancaster and then for the Totmonslow Hundred. At this period Shakespeare was writing plays and in 1587 Mary, Queen of Scots, had been executed following her detention, sometimes in Tutbury Castle, Staffordshire, and Wingfield Manor, Derbyshire. For many years Sampson Stubbs rode to the Quarter Sessions, where disputes were settled, crimes dealt with and licences issued for numerous ale houses. He witnessed statements, such as that given by a young man who made no complaint when boxed on the cheek for correction as a servant boy. The youth denied fighting with a gentleman of the Swythamley estate, in the parish of Leek. At the Manor Court of Church Lawton, Cheshire, Sampson Stubbs supervised the transference of the holdings of tenants and imposed fines on local offenders. Some of them had taken in lodgers, inmates and vagabonds, allowed their pigs to run free, or caused a nuisance by building a privy too close to the public highway. Sampson also presided at the Manor Court in part of Tunstall owned by the Earl of Bath until 1620, when a new owner discontinued the proceedings. Sampson Stubbs took clients to London Courts and some were indebted to him for his work on law suits, even to the time of his death. An early client was Edward Egerton Esq, of Wrinehill and £90 in fees were due for *'the prosecution by various suits'*. Sampson and his youngest son, held Basford

Bridge House at Cheddleton, near Leek, as security, and the debt was to be paid in instalments on certain Feast Days in the porch of Cheddleton Church. Perhaps this was a regular arrangement for the payment of dues. The Egertons owned Cheddleton Park and, in the 16th century, were in possession of a coalmine at Wrinehill, on the Cheshire border. Over one century later an Egerton relation, land-owning and titled, was to make an unimaginable change to the life of James Brindley.

Sampson Stubbs wrote his own will and described himself as a 'gentleman' with little worldly wealth. However, his house in Butterton had space for books and a study when such rooms were uncommon and few could read. There were two canopied beds and pieces of furniture regarded as heirlooms. In time and through her father, a great-granddaughter, Ruth Stubbs, inherited the Butterton property and two sparsely-furnished houses which may have been resting places for Sampson when out on business. One was at Thurlwood, in Astbury, Cheshire, and the other stood somewhere in Derbyshire.

Butterton, near Leek, Staffordshire

The executors of Sampson's will were his grandson of the same name and Sir Thomas Milward, of Eaton, in Derbyshire, the latter holding the office of Chief Justice of Chester. King Charles I (executed 1649) once spent the night at the home of Sir Thomas and so Sampson may have heard a first hand account of the King's visit. However, a soldier of the Royal Army kept a diary and noted that the dark and peaty moorland was a 'rebellious place'. During the Civil War, Sampson Stubbs and two other men of Butterton, one being John Stubbs, and all of a great age, were excused from making the journey to Stafford to give evidence on behalf of the villagers. Their statements were taken and read by the parson. Sampson Stubbs was most likely well over eighty years of age at his death in 1651. His will asked for burial with his wife and parents before his own pew in the chancel of Butterton Church.

Sampson's youngest son, named Ottewell and described as the 'prodigal son', sometimes assisted his father by collecting dues in the village and elsewhere. The second son, Henry, was educated at Broadgates Hall (later Pembroke College), Oxford, and in due course became the rector of Blore Ray, near Dovedale, during 1619. Henry remained there for the rest of his life, but died shortly before his father. Henry's son, Josiah, trained at Trinity College, Cambridge, and served at Blore occasionally, before induction as the rector of Kingsley in 1657. The induction took place without disturbance; the manner of the event being recorded as it was in the period of Cromwell's rule. Oliver Cromwell died in the following year. Josiah's second wife and his unmarried sister lived with him in Kingsley rectory. His son, by his first wife, was another Henry Stubbs. Young Henry appraised his father's possessions for probate purposes, putting a very high value on the books. Henry was a curate at Cheadle, Staffordshire, but he and his wife died young and childless.

Walter Stubbs, Sampson's eldest son, was a great-great-grandfather of James Brindley of canal fame. Walter suffered an early death in 1632 and his will described him as being of 'gentleman' status. Although living modestly and not come into his full inheritance, he owned more animals than his neighbours. Walter's widow, Ellen (née Dakin, of Hayes Gate, Warslow) and their children, Sampson, Richard, Matthew, Margaret, Ellen, Ann and Alice, would have been assisted and most likely influenced by Sampson senior. Sampson's views during the difficult Civil War period are unknown, but in 1656, some years after her grandfather's death, Alice married Henry Bowman, a yeoman of Alstonefield. As Captain Henry Bowman, he had been requested not to take up arms against the King.

In 1658, while her cousin Josiah Stubbs was the rector of Kingsley, Alice and her husband became Quakers. Bowman ancestors had been recorded in Alstonefield registers since 1544, as were the baptisms of the couple's two eldest sons. The first born died in infancy and Henry and Alice must have turned to the Religious Society of Friends in their sorrow. They joined some of the earliest members. Meetings were conducted without a creed, sacraments or priests and some displayed a religious fervour which led to the nickname 'Quakers'. There were many followers in the moorlands of North Staffordshire and the founder of the Society, George Fox of Fenny Drayton, Leicestershire, visited the homes of prominent members, including friends of the Bowmans.

In the early days there were often skirmishes, such as on the occasion when a Quaker missionary was pushed backwards off the high wall of Leek Parish Church into the street below and Quakers recorded that, *'His head broak'*. Meetings in private houses and large gatherings of people concerned the authorities so soon after the Civil War. Members were absent from services at the parish church and refused to pay tithes due to the clergy. These were punishable offences and the Bowmans and the family of Alice's sister, Ellen Buxton, were soon paying dearly for their actions. Ellen's husband, Simon, received 'manifold beatings'. Yet another aggravation to the authorities was that Quakers regarded everyone as equal and so refused to remove their hats in court, often remained silent and would not swear on oath. They obeyed only Christ.

James Brindley's grandmother was a child of Henry and Alice Bowman and she, named Elner/Ellin/Ellen, was born on 29 April 1661 a few days after the Coronation of Charles II. The baby's father was in Stafford Gaol for one year and seven months, his objection to paying tithes to the Church being regarded rather as the refusal to pay modern local taxes. In 1664 Alice became defiant and disturbed the Easter Day Holy Communion Service at St Edward's Church, in Leek. The commotion brought her ejection from the church, an appearance before 'one called a Justice' and a term in gaol until the next Quarter Sessions. This was followed by detention at the House of Correction, where she endured conditions that brought death to another child, her breast-fed baby, Matthew. His short life has not been entered on the pedigree chart here.

How these events affected little Ellen at the age of three years can only be imagined, but there was unfortunate tension between mother and daughter, even when Ellen had a husband and family of her own. No record of Ellen's marriage to Joseph Brindley has been found, but if she had married outside the Society of Friends, disownment would have followed. In 1687 Ellen Brindley, with her mother and eldest brother, witnessed a Quaker deed for a burial ground on Bowman land at Alstonefield, and so, presumably, Joseph and Ellen were both Quakers and married about the year 1683.

Alice Bowman, a widow since 1674, had spent many of her remaining years at Stockley Park and a brief record survives of her Quaker Meeting there. Alice's will was proven in 1690, when her moveable estate totalled £545. This enabled two sons to embark on new beginnings at Derbyshire granges, while her unmarried daughters received generous sums of money, perhaps as marriage portions. Ellen Brindley was the only daughter with a husband by that date and, although she had most likely received a settlement, she had troubles. Alice left Ellen £40 (£4000 now), a sum less than half her sisters' shares, but intended specifically for the maintenance of Ellen and her children. Most significantly, the money was to be held by Ellen's brother, Richard Bowman, and the will included the phrase *'except my daughter Ellen'* more than once. She was given security by her family, but she was controlled. Feelings must have run high, for Alice prevented the couple from going to court over the matter by stipulating that Ellen would lose her inheritance if she and her husband took such action. Noticeably, Alice did not name her son-in-law, her grandchildren, or even state her eldest daughter's surname. Had Ellen ceased to be a Quaker, or was there a clash of temperament? Maybe Ellen and her husband were unable to manage their affairs. The background and attitude of Ellen's husband, Joseph Brindley, must have had some bearing on the situation, but this research has not discovered his roots with certainty. There were several men named 'Joseph Brindley' in the district. The only family document to provide Joseph's name was the will of Ellen's cousin, Ruth Stubbs, who used the term 'now wife' for Ellen. This suggests that Joseph had been married previously and must have been a widower at the time of his marriage to

Ellen, divorce being virtually unknown. Neither the date nor the place of Joseph's burial has been found. Ruth Stubbs, of Butterton and Nottingham, spinster heiress to the Stubbs's property in Butterton, Derbyshire and Cheshire, knew of Ellen's problems and also left a legacy for her in the hands of Richard Bowman.

Richard, Alice Bowman's second surviving son, had been assisted by his mother in the purchase of a copyhold tenancy at Clay Lake, near Leek, but he spent time at Stockley Park, which was registered in his name as a Quaker Meeting house in 1701. His brothers, Henry and Cornelius, were able to establish themselves as tenants of large farms in Derbyshire, leaving Westwood, Leek, for Smerrill Grange and One Ash Grange, respectively. These ancient granges had been the medieval farms and grain stores of distant monasteries. As Quakers disapproved of outward show, the Bowmans maintained modest households, but they developed skills in large scale animal husbandry and increased in wealth, their prosperity being seen in the number and variety of animals. In 1714, Henry Bowman's estate of over £1,000 included wool worth £400 from over 1,000 sheep grazing with Henry's other animals on Smerrill and Harthill Moors. Cornelius Bowman settled at One Ash Grange, near Monyash, where his descendants became tenants of the Dukes of Devonshire of Chatsworth House for three hundred years. The grange lies above the dramatic landscape of Lathkill Dale and was once owned by the medieval monks of Roche Abbey, near Sheffield, when the isolation and hard life were considered suitable for disobedient members of their order. By 1748, another Henry, the son of Cornelius, owned and managed over 700 sheep, 28 cows, 3 bulls, several bullocks, 5 pigs, 40 goats and 23 horses. In addition, vast quantities of cheese were made and stored in hundredweights.

Alice Bowman's sons were not the first family connection with Derbyshire, for her sister Ann Stubbs had married John Roe, a yeoman of Parwich, in 1646. Some of the Roe children had tenants' rights at Roystone Grange, Ballidon, in the parish of Bradbourne, where its fascinating history has come to light in recent years through intensive archaeological research. Drystone walls, the floor of a Roman farmstead and a medieval monastic farm have been excavated close to the present farm buildings. Sampson Stubbs probably arranged the Roe marriage to his grand-daughter, for he had a *'loveing friend'* closely associated with the Roes of Parwich. However, there is no indication that the Roes maintained the relationship with the Quaker Bowmans living a few miles away, but the Bowman cousins may have visited the well-stocked ironmongery of Thomas Roe, a grandson of John and Ann Roe. The goods were in Ballidon, a deserted village for centuries, and possibly at Roystone Grange itself, with further stores in Winster. Ample supplies of hardware from harness to locks, foodstuffs such as dried fruits, sugars and spices, haberdashery, knitting needles, medicinal substances, paper and many useful items, were brought from near and far. Some came from abroad by sailing ship and then on strings of packhorses using tracks to the small communities in the hills. The ironmonger, a second cousin of James Brindley senior, died young and unmarried in 1717.

Further information concerning collateral lines of descent from the Bowman, Stubbs and Roe families are given here in the Postscript as some contributed to community life and to knowledge in the wider field. Meanwhile, this family history must return to Ellen Brindley, who settled with her husband and children at Stockley Park, Tutbury, in Staffordshire. In 1695, the Brindleys' youngest daughter, Prudence, was baptised at Tutbury Parish Church and the event seems to be the only register entry in which Joseph Brindley could be identified with certainty. Even Quaker events were to be recorded at this period, but Prudence was baptised, which is contrary to Quaker practice. In the following year, Richard Bowman's marriage to *'one of his holy sisters'*, Elizabeth Bentley, was noted in the Tutbury register and the childless couple may have been in the same household as the Brindleys until about 1707, when Richard's youngest sister, Alice, and her husband, Joseph Stevenson, came to farm large numbers of animals at Stockley Park. Richard and Elizabeth returned to the Leek and Cheddleton area, living at Old Basford alongside the Hammersley family, who had provided accommodation for George Fox, the founder of the Religious Society of Friends (Quakers).

It was common practice for young people to live and learn in the home of a relative and by 1714 the Brindleys' daughter, Esther, was at the home of Ellen's sister, Esther Bradford. The latter was married to Samuel Bradford, a Quaker yeoman many years her junior and from a farm at Wigginshill, Sutton Coldfield, Warwickshire. Consequently, it seems likely that Ellen Brindley's only son, James, later to become the father of the engineer, was placed with his senior uncle, Henry Bowman of Smerrill Grange, Youlgreave, Derbyshire, especially as James was *'of Youlgreave'* in the autumn of 1715.

Richard Bowman died six years before his sister Ellen Brindley, but he had managed her affairs well and made good provision for the Brindleys and other members of the Bowman family. By 1728, Richard had used Ellen's inheritance to purchase a house with a barn and three closes of land situated at Yoxall, for his sister and her unmarried daughter Prudence. Richard made a bequest of an additional two-acre plot and ensured sufficient burial money for Ellen. Yoxall and Stockley Park were both at gates into Needwood Forest and Ellen's eldest daughter, Hannah Linnis, lived at Anslow in the parish of Rolleston, also close to Stockley Park. Hannah had married Thomas Linnis at Rolleston Church in 1718. The Linnis family farmed on a much smaller scale than the Bowmans and Stevensons, and seem to have died out within a few decades. Ellen Brindley's second daughter, Esther Ludford, had married a Quaker at her Aunt Esther Bradford's house at Wigginshill and her husband, John Ludford, of Baddesley Ensor, Warwickshire, may have been a blacksmith. However, there were still tensions of some kind surrounding Ellen, so that James Brindley senior, her only son, was directed by Uncle Richard Bowman's will not to disturb his mother and sister Prudence at the Yoxall property.

Richard bequeathed two-thirds of a farm at Leek to his nephew James Brindley senior and referred to the farm called *'Lowe Hill Farm'* as *'my estate'*. The remaining third was left to Hannah Linnis, who must have enabled her brother to acquire her portion in 1729, for tradition has it that James purchased a share in that year. Brother and sister, James and Hannah, were to provide £2 and £1 respectively, each year, for the maintenance of their mother, who was left an additional £20 with payments at intervals. For some unknown reason, Richard controlled James by placing restrictions on him so that he would lose the farm for as long as he disturbed his mother and sister in Yoxall. Their homes were thirty miles apart. Accounts of the canal engineer's life claimed that his father was rather fond of gaming and taking part in country sports with those who were better off.

Prudence, supposedly living with her mother, aged thirty-four years and in receipt of her uncle's legacy, was most likely the 'Prudentia' Brindley married to George Walker at Burton-upon-Trent in 1729. Burton is close to Yoxall, Stockley Park and Anslow. Nothing more is known of Prudence, or the house in Yoxall, but if Prudence did not have children, the property was to be divided between James Brindley senior and his remaining sisters. Ellen Brindley's burial took place on the 19 January 1733/4 at Yoxall churchyard. It was probably attended by the very few family members left in the vicinity. If they had remained in the district, Hannah Linnis and Prudence would have been the only ones within walking distance. Apart from Esther, Ellen's children were not named after her family and it is easy to imagine that she was making a point when she chose the name Prudence for her youngest daughter. Ellen Brindley was the only Bowman of her generation not buried as a Quaker.

Ellen's sister, Ann, the first wife of Joseph Davison, the Quaker schoolmaster in Leek, had died long since. Another Quaker sister, Esther, was forty years old at her marriage to Samuel Bradford, a young yeoman farmer from Wigginshill, Sutton Coldfield. His infant half-brothers and half-sisters were to become prominent Quakers at Wigginshill, Birmingham and Tamworth, with close associations amongst well-known Midland Quakers (see Postscript). Ellen Brindley's youngest sister and her husband, Quakers Alice and Joseph Stevenson, had maintained a substantial farm at Stockley Park, but the widowed Alice returned to the vicinity of Leek. Her brother, Richard Bowman, had arranged accommodation and furniture for her at Old Basford, Cheddleton, alongside his widow.

As previously mentioned here, James, Ellen Brindley's only son, spent some boyhood years at Stockley Park and possibly time in agriculture with Uncle Henry Bowman at Smerrill Grange, Youlgreave. By the spring of 1714, Henry was buried in his own Quaker burial ground by Bowman's Barn at Alstonefield. In October 1715, James applied for a marriage licence at Chesterfield and was described on the marriage bond as an *'agricolam'* (agricultural worker) of *'Yolgrave'*. He may have hoped for a marriage in secrecy and haste at the parish church of Chesterfield, some fifteen miles from home. The church is a landmark famed for its twisted spire. Although aged thirty-one years, James made little preparation for a wedding and the ceremony was not allowed to proceed without the consent of parents or guardians. At this first attempt, James failed to take a friend or relative to complete the marriage bond and his bride-to-be, Susanna Bradbury, must have been under age. The pair waited until 25 January 1715/6, Susanna probably having a twenty-first birthday in the interval as parental consent was not attached to the bond. The ceremony was recorded in Latin: *'Jacobus Brindley de Paroch. de Yolgrave et Susanna Bradbury de Paroch. de Tiddeswall* [Tideswell]*'*

There were Bradbury families in Tideswell and at Great Rocks Dale before the newly wed couple settled at Tunstead nearby, but Susanna does not appear in Anglican or Quaker records for the area. The Brindleys' first born son, James, born later in 1716 and probably before 27 September, was to become the famous canal engineer. Several brothers and sisters were born at this isolated spot in the hills above Buxton and the family may have remained there until Richard Bowman made alternative arrangements for them. It is possible that Richard settled them at Lowe Hill Farm, Leek, well in advance of his death at the end of December 1727. Richard's will was proved in 1728, but his bequest of the farm to James Brindley senior and Hannah Linnis may have confirmed their rights to the property when the Brindleys were already in residence. By his will, Richard controlled the movements of the Bowman family to various homes or holdings - Alice to Old Basford, Cornelius to Catswall, near Leek, and so on.

The youngest child of James and Susanna Brindley was baptised 'Mary' at Leek Church in 1731 and from Lowe Hill the lives of the Brindleys' children began to take different paths. James left home to take an apprenticeship in millwrighting, Joseph became a millwright and eventually established his family at the Smelting Mill in Alton (Staffs), John was sent to Burslem to learn the art of potting, developed a business of some standing and eventually retired to Union Hall, Kinver (Staffs), while Henry became the miller at Danebridge Mill, in the parish of Leek and on the border with Cheshire. Although Henry did not continue in milling all his life, some of his descendants were millers in Cheshire and then in Mill Street, Leek.

The Brindleys' daughters and their husbands were Esther, Ann and Mary, married to Samuel Simcock, William Allen and Abraham Birchenall respectively. Samuel Simcock was a carpenter, married at Prestbury Church, Cheshire in 1749. He was an assistant of James Brindley before their introduction to canal engineering. William Allen was a Leek innkeeper with property in Tittesworth, while Abraham Birchenall/Birchenhough was from Wildboarclough ('Wilbercluff') in the local Cheshire hills. Married at Prestbury, Mary's future was safeguarded when the legacy from her father was to be held by her brother Henry.

In the days when families were self-sufficient there was little free time and a wise farmer made the most of warm days. The sporting interests of James Brindley senior were said to have interfered with the education of his children. However, in later chapters it will be seen that he had a greater interest in their future than has been thought. Tradition claims that Susanna made up for her husband's shortcomings as best she could, but no signature of Susanna has been found to indicate that she could write. Her husband was able to sign his marriage bond neatly and, in old age, he read his long will to witnesses. It was 1763 and James senior had little occasion to write. With ageing hands and eyes he ran out of space on the paper and omitted the 'l' from his name. James made the letter 'e' in the old way; very like an 'o' with a loop on top, as he had done on his marriage bond. His son James made his 'e' likewise. The will may have been written by James senior himself or by Thomas Smith, of the Lowe, who also signed as a witness and made similar large capital letters. Dorothy Smith, his widow, confirmed that she had often seen her husband's writing. Another witness was James Rowley, a bricklayer from Biddulph, called to repairs required at the farm. A photograph of a copy of the will, in different handwriting, has been deposited at the William Salt Library, Stafford. James Brindley senior lived for a few more years and his will was as follows:

In the Name of God Amen. I James Brindly [sic] of Low in the Parish of Leek in the county of Stafford yeaman [sic] do make this my last will and testement in mannor following that is to say I give and devis [devise] unto my wife Susanna during her life all my Mosinge [messuage] farm or tennement with the Lands and Appurtenances ther unto belonging and the titel thir of Sisuating and being in the Low afore sad [aforesaid] now in my possion [possession] during her Life and after her death I geve the same unto my son James Brindly and his Meal Ares [male heirs] for Ever Chargable with One Hundred and Fifty pounds & five Shilinge to be pad [paid] in mannor following that is to say the first twinty fift of march after my wifes deces [decease] to pay before he enters of the Estate In this mannor first I geve to my son Joseph the sum of thirty pounds to my son John the sum of thirty pounds to my daughter Asther [Esther] wife of Samuel Sinock [Simcock] thirty pounds, Ann Allian [Allen] wife of William Allian thirty pounds I have to my Son Hemrey [sic] the sum of Five Shilings, I forthemore devis in to my son Henreys hand the sum of thirty pounds in trust for my daghter [sic] Mary wife of Abreham Barchenall for Clothing and other Necesares What she wants to be pad [paid] to be pad as She plese to demand the same. I apint [appoint] my wife & my Son James Executors of this my Last Will. It is my will and plaser [pleasure] that my wife shall have my parsnell Esteat [personal estate] to pay my funeral Expences & my depts [debts] to her Selph in Witness wher of I have Set my hand and seal thes 19th of November 1763.

James Brindey [sic]

James Brindley senior left the farm to his widow and then for his son James after Susanna's death. Probate was delayed until 1773, after the death of James junior, but at the time of his father's death in 1770, the canal engineer was at the peak of his career. As an already overworked man with a serious health problem and a new young family, he had little time to attend to the affairs of his aged parents. James senior, about eighty-six years old, was buried in Leek churchyard, near the east end of the church from which his grandmother, Alice Bowman, had been arrested over one hundred years earlier. The Brindley gravestone, now very worn, may bear the date of burial as 6 August 1769, but the parish register records 6 August 1770. The same register notes the burial of 'Mary Brindley of ye Low Widow' on 2 October 1779. This must be a mistake for 'Susanna', as Brindley's descendants give the date of her death as 28 September 1779 (Campbell) and there is no other entry at that period. Both parents of James Brindley reached their mid-eighties in years and must have lived to know of the fame of their firstborn son.

CHAPTER 2
BEFORE CANALS

JAMES BRINDLEY
Millwright and Canal Engineer

Born 1716, son of James and Susanna Brindley, (nee Bradbury), at Tunstead, Wormhill, Derbyshire
Married 8 Dec 1765, at Wolstanton Parish Church, Ann(e) Henshall, bap 23 Apr 1747,
daughter of John and Anne Henshall, of Newchapel, Wolstanton, Staffordshire
Issue:
Ann(e), born 17 Dec 1769, bap 3 Jan 1770 at Newchapel, unmarried, died at sea, 1838
Susanna, born 6 Jan 1772, bap 27 Dec 1772 at Newchapel, died 17 Nov 1799
Married 8 Dec 1795 at Burslem Parish Church, John Bettington of St James', Bristol, merchant
Issue:
James Brindley Bettington b 1796
John Henshall Bettington b 1798

Died 27 Sep 1772 at Turnhurst, Newchapel, Wolstanton; bur 30 Sep 1772, Newchapel.
Probate 18 Dec 1772 (Adm.)

James Brindley's early years in the Derbyshire hills and the Staffordshire moorlands, with their bogs, rocks and rivers, stood him in good stead for the outdoor life ahead. His brothers and sisters were very close to him in age and he must have experienced the rough and tumble of family life, with a harassed mother and a father struggling to cater for their large family. Self-sufficiency was usual at that period. Animals on their small-holding required constant care and the young sons helped with menial tasks as farmers' children do. This enabled their father to take some time off for sporting pleasures. Maybe this was in excess, but who can be certain? Children made their own amusements in those days and young James was said to have enjoyed whittling wood with a knife and had an interest in mechanical things. Country boys often carried a knife as a useful tool, toys were rare and whittling was something they did. The *Gentleman's Magazine* of the period described how Samuel Roe, of Bakewell, built a frame in the church to protect large memorials from the rough hands and knives of boys. Until James reached the age of seventeen, it may have been taken for granted that he, as the eldest son, would take on Lowe Hill Farm. About the year 1730, ten-year-old John, the third son, was sent to Burslem to learn the art of potting, but nothing else is known of his brothers at that time.

The Brindley household was not Quaker and it is impossible to know to what extent James senior associated with his mother's relatives on his return to Leek. It was and is a small market town, but the Quakers were a close-knit society, travelling here and there to a network of meetings and the homes of devout members. Joseph Davison, a mercer, was the Quaker schoolmaster in Leek. He was a great-uncle of young James Brindley by Joseph's marriage to Ann Bowman, but she died before 1711 and Joseph Davison was married twice more before his death in 1747. There is no indication that young James attended the Quaker school, although at one time the

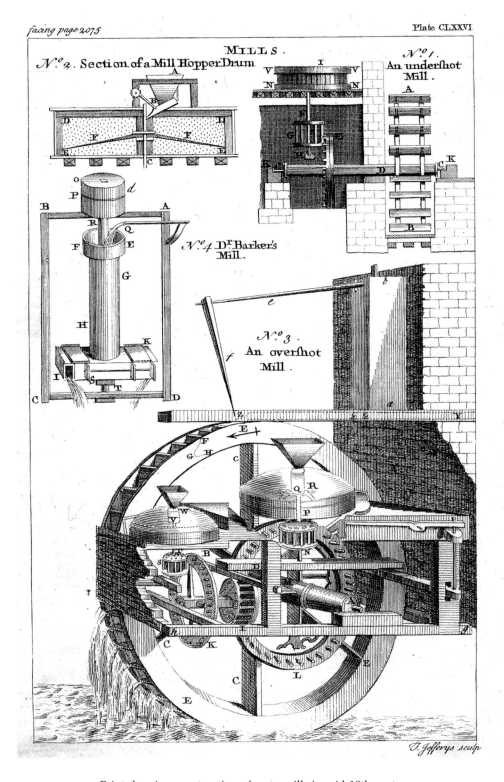

Print showing construction of watermills in mid-18th century

Views of Leek Mill between modern factories

Leek Mill, built by James Brindley. Part was removed for road widening

Society had agreed to admit the children of non-Quakers.

On 19 January 1733/4, in the spring of 1734 by the modern calendar, young James's seventy-four year old grandmother Ellen Brindley was buried in Yoxall. It is likely that James had never met her, for he was born over forty miles away and his father was restrained from disturbing her at Yoxall by the will of Uncle Richard Bowman. The turning point in James Brindley's life came about after his grandmother's death, for he was the eldest son of her only son. She did not leave a will, Richard Bowman having settled everything in advance, but her maintenance payments from James Brindley senior and Hannah Linnis, his sister, would cease. If their sister Prudence was childless and no longer alive, the Yoxall property was to be divided between James senior and his two remaining sisters. Tradition has it that young James began an apprenticeship in millwrighting in 1733, but in the old calendar 1733 ended on 24 March 1734 and so it seems feasible that James left Lowe Hill sometime between 19 January and 24 March 1734, when he was still seventeen years old. Davenport wrote in 1841 that the profession of millwrighting had a high standing and a *'considerable premium'* may have been paid, or the young man had shown talent already.

James left Lowe Hill Farm and journeyed northward to the business of Abraham Bennett at Gurnett in Sutton, in the ancient Cheshire parish of Prestbury. For ten miles the old road from Leek led over the hills and across Danebridge, where the young River Dane forms the county boundary, but the hills become even higher before the track drops down to Sutton, a village close to Macclesfield. Although there is as yet no proof, James's mother may have had connections with the area. The will and inventory of a John Bradbury, dated 1699, recorded that he was a miller of Bosley (see Appendix).

Towards Wildboarclough above the Dane valley

Early accounts tell how James Brindley took some time to settle in Bennett's workshop and had problems fixing the spokes of a wheel, but he was soon in a position to make good repairs and even improve machinery when others failed. The youth's confidence grew as he learned skills involving work with rivers, wheels and machinery for silk and paper mills. By the age of nineteen years, James Brindley had solved problems with the machinery of a Macclesfield silk mill and, while still in his apprenticeship, redesigned and built the new machinery for a paper mill by the River Dane. For a century or so, the exact location of the corn mill then being converted to a paper mill has been debateable. However, Mr Tony Bonson's recent research concludes that the paper mill in question was Wincle (Whitelee) Mill, although there is little more than the weir remaining at the site on the Cheshire bank below Danebridge. James's master had failed to complete the necessary work there, but the young man was said to be so keen that he walked to Manchester and back (25 miles each way) during one weekend, in order to study another machine, find out how it was done and memorise the details. Work on simple repairs produced a demand for Brindley's workmanship and Abraham Bennett began to realise the value of his apprentice, leaving him to continue with little supervision. Some 130 years later, Samuel Smiles wrote that colleagues and even Abraham Bennett had held the view that, '...*there will be very little trade left to be done when thou comes oot o' thy time: thou knaws firmness o' wark's th' ruin o' trade'.* Smiles, a Scot who had worked in Leeds, gave Bennett an accent and dialect from much further north than east Cheshire. A short 'thay/thee' is still often used for 'you', and 'youer' for 'your', but 'oot' would not have been heard for 'out'. Frequently, James was left in charge before his apprenticeship was completed and he continued in the business after his master's death for the benefit of the Bennett family until all was wound up. It was 1742 and he was twenty-six years old.

It is generally believed that James Brindley returned to the town of Leek, where his father farmed on the southern side of the town. James would be strong to build mills and dress the heavy millstones. Carpentry, masonry and metalwork were essential skills. He is thought to have set up a workshop and gained valuable experience repairing equipment and visiting clients over a wide area. At some point he began to rebuild Leek Mill, by the River Churnet, at the bottom of Mill Street.

Even so, Mr T Bonson's research into the history of the mills situated by the River Dane shows that the father of James Brindley has been much maligned by reports of his disinterest in his children's education and livelihood. Documentary evidence shows that James senior leased part of Danebridge Mill for six months on 22 October 1742, the year his son left the Bennett family. He took possession of the rest by lease and release on 19 March 1742/3 (old Calendar) for £100. The mill was situated on the Staffordshire side of the river and close to the bridge young James had crossed many times on his walk to and from Abraham Bennett's workshop. Although the occupancy changed from time to time through letting, Brindleys were involved with Danebridge Mill for over one hundred years, while some held properties in and around Mill Street, Leek, from time to time.

Consider the family situation in the 1740s. The parents, James and Susanna

Brindley, had been at Lowe Hill Farm from about 1726 and were there for the rest of their lives. Their eldest son had completed his apprenticeship as a millwright and was becoming skilful with machinery, but what of his brothers? Nothing is known of an apprenticeship for Joseph and he may have worked with James briefly. By 1764, Joseph called himself a millwright in Alton, but at the time of his marriage there in 1746, he was described as *'a yeoman of the parish of Cawdon* [Cauldon?]*'*. A yeoman was someone who held land, even if only a smallholding. John, the third son, continued his career in potting. By 1742 young Henry was about seventeen years old, the age to begin an apprenticeship as young James had done. Would their father have rented the large premises at Danebridge Mill for the untrained Henry? It is likely that the mill was intended for James, Joseph and Henry. James senior would have realised the potential in a property with a house and mills for corn, paper and fulling, although the latter process for cleansing and thickening woollen cloth was discontinued and the site run down. James had already shown his skill at the paper mill a short distance away. Perhaps his father thought he could manage a family partnership. Danebridge Mill was in Heaton, in the chapelry of Rushton Spencer and in the huge parish of Leek, although the town was seven miles away as the crow flies.

In time, the Brindley sons went their own way and it is difficult to estimate the success of the business. If Henry had been instructed by his brother James with a formal or informal apprenticeship, his seven years would have ended in 1749/50. James would have expected to travel here and there repairing tools and machinery as a millwright, and he would have seen that Danebridge Mill was in good order. However, it seems significant that in 1750 he was free to rent a workshop in Burslem. His brother John knew many people in the neighbourhood of the ancient village and James Brindley was able to rent premises from the Wedgwood family. This move began the friendship between the twenty-year-old Josiah Wedgwood and the thirty-four-year-old millwright.

Leek Mill was not forgotten as James began to rebuild it. Chiselled into a wall at first floor level is TI 1752 JB. TI is thought to be Thomas Joliffe, the landlord, using the old style interchangeable I and J. Thomas Joliffe was of Mosslee and Whitehough, the latter having been the mansion of the Quaker Mellor family and where a relation of the Bowmans was married at a Quaker Meeting. James Brindley may have worked on Leek Mill over a long period before 1752 as the property was much larger than the present remaining section. He was busy earning a living and probably worked on his own project in spare time, but his surviving notebooks beginning in 1753 show he had little of that. The jottings give no indication whether Leek town, Danebridge or Burslem was regarded as his home. He named workmen and mills where he carried out repairs or gave advice, and occasionally mentioned lodgings, inns, or board provided by a client.

There were several mills in the Leek area, but the mill at the bottom of Mill Street had been worked by a Brindley family before 1571, for that is the date of probate on the will of Randle Brundle/Brundley/Brindley. He had the mill, a smithy and four sons named William, Lawrence, Thomas and Elias/Ellis (see Appendix). The mill was William's inheritance, but there is no reference to it in papers surviving from the

17th century. Craftsmen were often members of the same family and Leek parish registers show Brindleys and their relations were in carpentry, masonry and blacksmithing. Documents concerning the smithy inherited by Lawrence mention a man named Joseph in the family, but there is no proof that he was James Brindley's grandfather. There were other 'Josephs' in the district, one being a Quaker.

James Brindley's Mill at Leek

Modern factory buildings have been omitted

From this period onwards, James Brindley became involved in larger projects while maintaining his reputation in attending to local business. Tradition has it that Brindley's name was mentioned at a wedding celebration in 1750, when the owner of a coalmine told of flooding in Wet Earth Colliery at Clifton, between Manchester and Bolton. The books of Smiles and Meteyard gave inaccurate details of the wedding, but John Ward, writing his *History of the Borough of Stoke-upon-Trent*, correctly named the bride and groom as Rachel Edensor and Michael Heathcote, who married at Hartington, on the Derbyshire border. The Lancashire mine owner was John Heathcote, the uncle of the bridegroom. Brindley's drainage system was a success.

The project at Wet Earth Colliery involved the construction of Ringley Weir and eight hundred yards of tunnelling. Two shafts were sunk to complete an inverted siphon and a huge water wheel in an underground chamber was built to operate the pumps. All was designed with consideration of the mine and the bed of the River Irwell. The work took four years. Such a scheme had not been done before and books referred to in the text here should be read for the technical details. It is believed that only a few men worked on the tunnelling with the primitive tools of that period, while James Brindley continued with other work. The scheme made slow progress between 1752 and 1756, but it was entirely successful and, according to Thomas Bentley, '...it ensured Brindley's supremacy', for he had 'erected a very extraordinary water engine'. During the 1960s AG Banks and RB Schofield, two professional engineers, explored the Wet Earth Colliery site with the help and encouragement of local people. Their survey of the remnant of Brindley's work concluded that he was 'a brilliant intuitive and practical engineer', and, in their opinion, modern engineers would have to have 'a good deal of native invention to deal with the problems as Brindley did'. They even used the same adjective as Thomas Bentley - 'extraordinary'.

In 1961, a sluice gate from a wash-out tunnel in the construction was found during excavations for a sewerage scheme near Kearsley Power Station. The site was close to Ringley Weir and on the opposite bank of the River Irwell to the power station, which has made use of Brindley's weir during this century. The old hand-hewn gate of oak was left in the open for two years before being taken to Smithills Museum, Bolton, for safekeeping. Again, in 1963, a second gate of different dimensions and in a poorer condition was taken to the Science Museum in London. The first gate had a shaft, twelve feet in height, with six horizontal panels placed one above the other to a height of over five feet, while the second gate had seven panels and was narrower. Brindley would have known of the ancient design from his river work, but both had sound iron bolts and plates, which had retained 'a good condition'. The large underground wooden waterwheel at the Wet Earth development lasted until 1867, when new equipment was installed. The chamber was filled in during 1964 and much of the intact tunnelling, including that under the river, was sealed for safety reasons.

The next major operation took Brindley to the construction of a silk mill in Congleton. Work began in 1755, but he was only required to attend to the larger wheels of the machinery, while another man was in charge of the smaller wheels and the whole installation. It soon became obvious to the owners and to Brindley that the other man was not up to the task. The man became annoyed and uncooperative when the mill owner suggested that Brindley should assist him. He spitefully refused to allow Brindley an examination of the plans of the whole machine and gave him just a few parts to work on. By this time, Brindley was frustrated and insisted angrily that he could complete the whole installation without interference. This request was granted, putting him in a position to add improvements which eventually benefited machines used in the cotton industry. Davenport mentioned the *'contrivance'* for winding bobbins equally instead of in wreaths and another for stopping the machinery of the whole mill or just part of it. Brindley also devised a method of cutting teeth and pinion wheels in a less laborious way, which reduced costs. Unfortunately, Brindley's surviving notebooks do not record any of this.

Few of Brindley's writings are easily available, but a photostat copy of one of his notebooks covers an important period of his life. It shows the transition from routine work with mills, shafts and foundations to advisory work at Congleton silk mill, his first commission to install an engine and the initial survey for a canal through Staffordshire. The simple entries give no hint of the excitement Brindley must have felt at being asked to become involved in the latter pioneering scheme.

Brindley's notebooks have been considered difficult to read for a number of reasons. Primarily they were memoranda, nothing more than 'jotters' and occasionally written in the careless manner of private notes. They were never meant as complete, chronological accounts for the eyes of others. The notebook dated 1755-1758 generally relates to the time taken on particular projects, the charges or expenses incurred, plus a few random jottings. Phonetic spelling reflecting the local speech was common at that period; vowel sounds were variable, dictionaries were rare and schooling limited. Brindley used the abbreviation 'te', with a raised 'e', for 'the', his old style 'e' was easily mistaken for an 'o' and the quality of his writing varied with the thickness of the quill pen - the finer the nib, the neater the writing. Numbers were formed correctly and the setting out of his simple accounts and an occasional calculation suggest that he must have had some instruction.

The 1755-1758 notebook began with, '*Two days at Congletoun* (Congleton) *a bout te silk mill advising'*, a service for which Brindley charged 2s a day. His estimate or charge for a job was given by the number of days involved, generally at a rate of 2s per day at the beginning of the book, 2s 6d in 1756 and 3s a day for '*prescribeing'* on 12 September 1758. Presuming that Brindley worked for six days a week through the year, the latter sum would have produced £46 16s per annum, having risen from £31 4s in 1755. By comparison, his distant family connections, beginning their careers as young clergymen in Derbyshire, received less than Brindley's earnings. In 1754, the curate of Bradbourne was paid £20 a year and, in 1763, his brother's salary rose to £40 per annum on appointment as the curate in fashionable Ashbourne. In 1755, one and a half day's carpentering by Sam. Simcock, Brindley's brother-in-law, cost 1s 9d, a rate of 1s 2d per day or £18 4s per annum. An undated page showed that labourers earned one shilling a day (£15 12s per annum). Of course, these are not full accounts and the cost of running Brindley's premises is not known, but he occasionally noted charges for a horse. On 17 May 1756, his expenses for a day spent with '*Mr Bucknall for Hors Hire and myself'*, were 3s 6d. In 1757, he paid £1 5s 8d for his '*Hors at grass'* for 80 days and 7s 6d for 53 days winter pasture. By 27 June 1758, while looking out timber, his '*Charges and waiges* [sic] *Self and Hors'* were 5s. Other small sums and jottings included 1s 8d for lath nails, the purchase of files and steel, the receipt of 213 feet of '*older'* boards, or '*alder'* boards, from Thomas Bryan. Alder wood is durable in water. On 3 May 1757, Brindley paid 10s '*for B[P]arish money'* perhaps the parish rate.

Already forty years old, Brindley was becoming mindful of his health and he noted a page of remedies to ease '*the gravel or stone'*, the ague or a shivering with fever, and a '*payn'* in the back. A pound of new lime boiled in a gallon of water was recommended for the first problem and, when the mixture cleared, a pint was to be taken three times a day - '*mak more if a Cagen recuire* [if occasion require]'. Drinking your own urine when warm was the suggested remedy for ague, but this was not unusual when people were willing to try anything in the days before modern medicine. Back pain could be relieved by making a '*seer* [sear] *cloth'* from a heat producing mixture of '*oxocrothe'* [oxycroceum or oxycrate saffron or a mixture of vinegar and water?], cardamom [a spice usually for settling the stomach], diacodium [a syrup of poppy heads (opiate) in honey] and leathery parasol mushrooms. All were boiled to the consistency of a '*Ruptar* [rupture] *plaster'* and applied to the affected area.

Brindley jotted a reminder that 6 August 1758 was '*Stoak waks'* (Stoke Wakes), the local holiday and fair, when there was much drinking. There is no sign that James Brindley enjoyed a day in Stoke, but he paid two workmen for seven weeks' work. Brindley's notebook named workmen and people he met in the course of business. He called on a millstone maker in Nottingham, a tanner, a '*Breek Laar'* [bricklayer] and people in Newcastle-under-Lyme. Later, he went for '*iorn'* at the same town, where the main street is known as The Ironmarket. Brindley worked for Mr '*fillep'* Antrobus of Congleton, for Mr Tibbets of Trentham, for Mr '*Grifis'* [Griffiths] at New Inn Flint Mill and searched for timber with Mr Yates of Halmerend, near Audley. He met millers and millwrights - '*Snaip* [Snape] *the mill-Right'* at Bucknall Flint Mill at a

Extracts from James Brindley's notebook

cost of 2s 6d, Mr George Goodwin of Monyash for Ashbourne Mill, Mr Kent's corn mill at '*Codan*' [Cauldon?], Wheelock's Mill, Abbey Hulton Mill, Nottingham Mill, Marchant Brookes's Flint Mill and Mr John Baddles [Baddeley's] Flint Mill. Shafts were examined at Brown Edge and elsewhere and foundations surveyed for George Critchlow at Pethills, near Leek. Brindley then attended to a stop-cock and altered a pump for Earl Gower at Trentham. Nevertheless, Brindley gave little detail whether he repaired a mill or felled a big tree, but contrary to popular belief, he drew plans occasionally. On 19 and 23 March 1757, he wrote, '*draing a plann*', for which he charged 2s 6d on the first occasion and 4s on the second, when the service was coupled with the setting out of a wheel race.

On 1 December 1755, Brindley searched for timber at Bradley Ash and in Oker Woods, near Ashbourne, in preparation for the construction of Mr Goodwin's mill. At a cost of 7s 6d for three days, Brindley made sure there was suitable timber available in the area. Later, he repaired the boards on Hanging Bridge over the River Dove, but the work at the mill began in March 1756 and the millwright was still paying for accommodation in Ashbourne in 1757. The first period totalled just over 57 days at the mill, with a further eight days spent on the floodgates. The second stage, in 1757, concerned the building of the internal mechanism, the flour mill. Brindley recorded his estimate of the number of days required and those taken, but he underestimated, as so often happens with outdoor work. On 1 July 1756, he received £41 9s 10d from Mr Goodwin of Monyash, with extra sums for workmen - Thomas Pearson, Thomas Ball, John Thorneycroft and Sanders - making £47 11s 6d. On two occasions, Brindley paid Dorothy/Dole [Dolly] Marton/Marten for '*bord*', presumably in Ashbourne - sums of £1 17s 6d on 19 September 1756 and for '*67 days in full of all a £1 13s 6d on 2 July 1757*'. It seems the rate for a night's lodging was 6d. Ann Goodwin of Leek was another woman named in Brindley's notebook as he had lent her 5s and then 10s during the autumn of 1756.

Although busy with corn mills and routine work, Brindley developed an interest in engines. On 31 March 1756, he set out to visit a forge in Cheshire, taking three days at 3s a day and, on two occasions, rode to Bakewell where boiler plates were being made. It has been thought that Brindley inspected Newcomen engines while on a journey to Bedworth, Warwickshire, but his notes were confined to the expenses incurred on the way. On 27 April, he spent 2s 9d in Lichfield, with an extra 10d for two new shoes, presumably for his horse. He dined at Coleshill for 9d on the following day and wrote '*Coosill*', almost as it is pronounced locally. At Bedworth he noted 2s for his visit as well as 3s 2d expenses for himself and his horse. Brindley had journeyed there for '*Drilling*' and as the area had coal and iron, it seems possible that his advice was requested following his success at Wet Earth Colliery. The visit was brief and he returned to Fenton via Birmingham and Wolverhampton without comment.

Brindley was installing an engine at Little Fenton for Mr Broad and wrote without a date that his '*Dabts oing* [Debts owing] *of the Engon a Count/Coolbrook Daal* [Coalbrookdale] *Du* [due] *£28 9s*', with sums for Mr Edensor of Congleton, Cheadle for brass, stones from Congleton, to '*Ginder*' for iron and '*for Carige from Collbrook*' [carriage from Coalbrook]. Brindley recorded the days he spent on the Little Fenton engine - the *'sillender, brass from Cheadle'* and *'fenton Housesort out* [sort out the engine house]', for example, but on 1 August these entries were followed by an inexplicable note - *'fenton no money 4 day'* - and dashes under the account although no sums of money had been entered. Mr Broad was not mentioned again until a meeting on 3 October and further contact in the following year, when Brindley appeared to be paying Mr Broad. In the spring of 1757, he paid 11s *'upon Mr Broad a Count to John Mathes* [Mather?]' and 1s 10d *'pad Mr Broad for Bord'*. A series of payments were made to John and, occasionally, to Mary *'Mathes'*. In May, Brindley noted the measurements of four *'scantlings'* or rafters, 8 feet by 6 inches by 4 inches for a corbel, or truss, probably for the Broads' coal-pit at Fenton, where an engine was to be built for Miss Broad.

Engine work required visits to Coalbrookdale, Shropshire, where the Darby family had won fame for their ironwork. They used coke for smelting, bringing improvements to iron products at the very beginning of the Industrial Revolution. Abraham Darby II, a Quaker, had been in business for some decades and was visited from time to time by Henry Bradford, a Quaker from Birmingham. Quakers were keen on establishing credentials about themselves as they moved from one Meeting to another and it is likely that the Darbys knew that Brindley's Aunt Esther Ludford had lived in the household of Henry Bradford's childhood home. Henry was the much younger half-brother of Brindley's deceased great-uncle Samuel Bradford, of Wigginshill, near Sutton Coldfield. Samuel had married Esther Bowman at the Leek Meeting in 1705. James Brindley may not have known them, but there were other Leek connections, for Abraham Darby II and his wife Abiah were friends of Quaker Joshua Toft of Haregate Hall, Leek, where the couple first met (Rachel Labouchere, 1988). Haregate was a quaint, gabled, Dutch-looking house, according to Sleigh's history of the town of Leek. The occupants, Joshua and John Toft, associated with Brindley's Quaker relatives and travelled with them to the Stafford Meeting. In 1711 the Tofts' sister Ruth became the second wife of Joseph Davison, the Quaker schoolmaster and great-uncle of James Brindley by Davison's first marriage.

In 1745, Joshua Toft, a manufacturer of buttons, encountered Highland officers when Prince Charles Edward Stuart, 'Bonnie Prince Charlie', led Scottish soldiers over the moors into Leek. Toft, being a peaceable Quaker, invited officers into his home on the condition that they left their weapons outside, but the tired and hungry army marched on plundering for food and supplies. Joshua's little daughter was lifted onto the shoulders of a soldier to see her 'King' pass through the market place, while townsfolk - and possibly James Brindley - protected their property.

Joshua Toft had attended to Quaker business and weddings in Shropshire for some years before James Brindley rode to Coalbrookdale thinking of engines. In 1757, James began work on the engine for Miss Broad at Fenton Vivian - another 'fire-engine' as such engines were called. In February, stones and mortar were brought and a visit to Coalbrookdale followed in March. The making of pipes continued until the end of April, when the engine-house work began, necessitating another journey to Coalbrookdale. During May, Brindley attended to the engine-house, burning brass and *'Rearing the sillender* [sic]'. In June, he formed piston hoops, gave further attention

Haregate Hall mid-19th century

to the engine house and, in July, fixed a *'Grat Leaver* [great lever]', presumably the beam and piston rods. From 17 July to 21 August, he was *'about the boiler'*, and spent two days at the end of August visiting Wrexham, a mining area. He attended to mills during the same period, going *'with tools'* on 17 August and supervising the first turning of a mill wheel before setting out for Wrexham on 31 August 1757. The pumps, the *'copson* [capstan]' and the pit for the engine occupied him in September. Brindley considered the time required by each process and, on the other side of a wavering line, noted the actual time taken. He estimated 82 days for work that took 95 days. And then there was luck - *'bad'*, and *'middlin'*. Through December 1757, the work *'about the sestern* [cistern]' continued and, on 26 February 1758, Brindley noted that he *'intanded* [intended] *to a have set te Engon to work'*. It worked for ten days in March and again into April for another seven days. By 9 April the engine must have been put to good use for a *'Deep wind boor* [deep bore by winding]' was made, presumably at the Broads' Fenton colliery, and a *'sack of coals was sold'*. By 16 April 1758, the project was declared to be *'in good order'*. There was no mention of Miss Broad at this time, but on Wednesday 1 March 1758, Brindley received the sum of £71 11s 6d *'to te Engon a Count from Mr Tho Hentrell'*, possibly her agent.

An unidentified project required payments to named workmen, a number of labourers and sawyers, to which account Brindley added 1s 6d for himself as he *'ran about a Drinking'*. Perhaps the work had been completed to his satisfaction. Brindley was constructing flint mills, but the dust from the ground flint for the pottery industry was a health hazard and so the process took place under water. Eliza Meteyard described a windmill built by Brindley for grinding flint to supply the pottery of John and Thomas Wedgwood, at Burslem. She told of the large sails falling at the initial operation, but adjustments corrected the situation and the strong building gave decades of service. Cheddleton Flint Mill, now open to the public, is not an example of Brindley's work.

In 1843, John Ward described a mill built by Brindley on land near Tunstall, where it pumped water from a coal mine and ground flint for potters. In 1812, unusual features were disclosed at its demolition. For example, '... *the pump trees, which were wooden staves bound together with ashen hoops, were found to be lined with cow hides, the working buckets being also covered with leather, a strange contrivance'*. On 16 May 1757, James Brindley recorded the payment of £2 6s for two hides, without reference to their purpose or the project. '*The mine-shaft was more than two hundred yards distant from the mill; and, to work the pumps, he invented slide-rods, which were moved horizontally by a crank at the mill, and gave power to the upright arm of a crank-lever, whose axis was at the angle, and the lift at the other extremity.'* Mr T Baddeley, of a local family, believes the site was near the old Whitfield Colliery in Norton-in-the-Moors and part of the manor of Tunstall. In 1771, a large scale parish map was drawn by John and Hugh Henshall, father and son. It clearly shows a scheme that would drain underground water from the colliery and it fits Ward's description exactly. The Engine Meadow and the Water Engine are shown, with symbols indicating the slide-rods and pump. Mr Baddeley suggests that the 200 yards of slide-rods, drawn to scale, '*...were resting on the ground in a trough up the valley side, while the Water Engine would have the flint mill from which William Clowes removed the crushing stampers in 1800. There was a saw mill near the top of the run of slide-rods, where the pump and drainage shaft were located; possibly using the same power source.'* The mill leat was on Foxley Brook. Brindley noted a visit to shafts at Brown Edge nearby.

Although Brindley's construction had unique features, he may have called on Quaker Joseph Whitfield at Bower's Hall, a mere two miles south of Bakewell, and not many more from Brindley's Quaker cousins. Joseph Whitfield was not connected with the Staffordshire colliery of the same name, but was the agent for the Quaker owned London Lead Company with mines in Darley and Winster. He was a friend of Abraham Darby and mentioned a crank to Darby in 1748. By 1756, the Mill Close mine in Darley had '*sixteen yards of slide connecting rods'* in use (Raistrick, 1953, 1970). Brindley went to Bakewell for boiler plates on two occasions in the same year. The exchange and duplication of ideas was to be expected as the problems were similar, but Brindley's 200 yards of slide-rods were more ambitious than the 16 yards at the Mill Close mine. Raistrick suggested that the friendship between Brindley and Whitfield, with other Quakers, enabled Brindley to gain the appointment as engineer of the Leeds and Liverpool Canal fourteen years later.

'*Upon a windey day'*, 15 March 1757, Mr John Baddeley and the millwright Brindley visited '*Matherso'*. This may be Mathers/Matthews or an unidentified place, where at least a new mill wheel was required. Moddershall, where the valley had several mills, has been suggested as a likely site. Brindley drew plans and set out the wheel-race. Despite coming up against rock, by July and August the wheel was attended to '*with tools'* and turned thirteen days later. On 22 February 1758, Brindley '*began to work the Engen for Mr John Baddles* [Baddeley's] *flint mill'*, and he incorporated a '*niew invention'* at Mr Griffith's New Inn flint mill during the summer of the same year. Brindley attended for two days and then checked the progress each month -

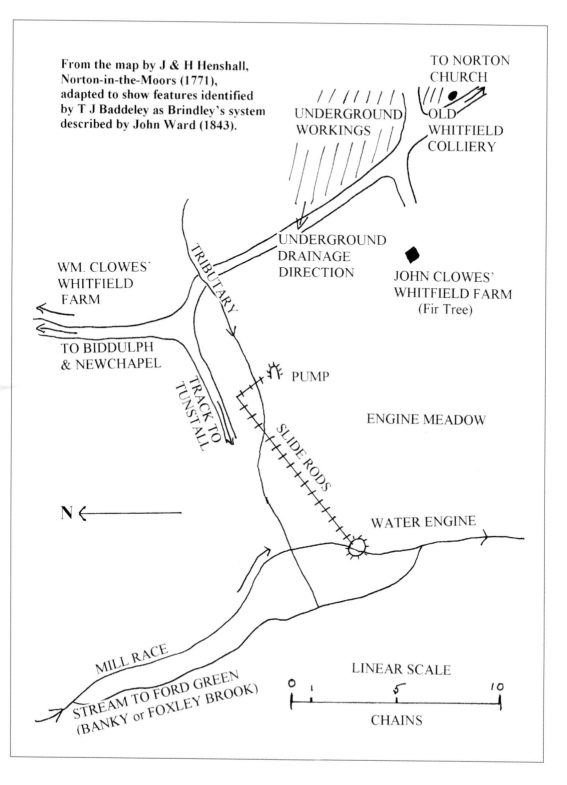

From the map by **J & H Henshall,
Norton-in-the-Moors (1771),**
adapted to show features identified
by **T J Baddeley** as Brindley's system
described by **John Ward (1843).**

TO NORTON
CHURCH

UNDERGROUND
WORKINGS

OLD
WHITFIELD
COLLIERY

UNDERGROUND
DRAINAGE
DIRECTION

WM. CLOWES'
WHITFIELD
FARM

TRIBUTARY

JOHN CLOWES'
WHITFIELD FARM
(Fir Tree)

TO BIDDULPH
& NEWCHAPEL

TRACK TO TUNSTALL

PUMP

ENGINE MEADOW

SLIDE RODS

N

WATER ENGINE

MILL RACE

STREAM TO FORD GREEN
(BANKY or FOXLEY BROOK)

LINEAR SCALE

0   1   5   10

CHAINS

Part of map of Norton-in-the Moors (Henshall, 1771), with additions by T. Baddeley about the foundation, the brickwork, the pan and the finishing. Unfortunately, he did not define the invention.

The last dated entry in the notebook was for *'prescribeing'* on 12 September 1758, but the jottings had become miscellaneous. They included the numbers of bricks for foundations, an engine-house pit and a *'fyer stool'*, while on another page were the specifications of a *'stoves sillender'* to be made with an inside diameter of 16 inches and an inside height of 20in. A *'bodey pipe'* of 5in. diameter and others of 5^1/2in and 4 in diameters were also needed. Another calculation referred to a 42in cylinder. Brindley built an experimental engine for himself, incorporating wood, but he travelled to Coalbrookdale for other parts. Mr Spedding, of Whitehaven, wrote a full description of this engine for William Brown, an engineer of Newcastle-upon-Tyne, making reference to *'Brindley's Machine'* from Coalbrookdale records. In 1763, *'a most complete and noble piece of ironwork'* was erected at the Walker Colliery, on Tyneside. Smiles claimed it as Brindley's work but Raistrick mentioned that Brindley visited Coalbrookdale when the unique engine was being made.

In December 1758, Brindley patented his early steam engine (Pat. No.730):

'A Fire Engine for Drawing Water out of Mines, or for Draining of Lands, or for Supplying of Cityes; Townes; or Gardens with Water, or which may be applicable to many other great and usefull [sic] Purposes, in a better and more effectual Manner than any Engine or Machine that hath hitherto been made or used for the like Purpose'.

Brindley was familiar with the properties of wood as a poor conductor of heat, but this early success was short-lived, although the famous James Watt also used wood in his early experiments. Brindley's memoir, written by Thomas Bentley, thought the millwright's *'...various other contrivances ...would probably have brought the steam engine to a greater degree of perfection, if a number of obstacles had not been thrown in his way by some interested engineers, who strenuously opposed any improvements they could not call their own'.* Obviously, there was an atmosphere of petty jealousy among those who hoped to be 'first'.

On 9th September 1759, Mr William Brown wrote a letter concerning Brindley's engine. He described his visit to see the engine at Fenton and then to Coalbrookdale with the intention of meeting James Brindley. Mr Brown and a Mr Walton set out from Newcastle-upon-Tyne on the 28th August 1759 and arrived in Newcastle-under-Lyme, Staffordshire, on the night of the 31st. They hoped to see everything about the Fire Engine built by Mr Brindley, *'without any hindrance from any of his people'.* When they arrived, Mr Broad told them that Brindley had gone to Coalbrookdale to build a boiler there. Mr Broad willingly took them to see his engine, but would not let them see inside the boiler, *'...he was upon the Reserve as to that point. However we soon learned how it was constructed by Dint of money we gave the men to Drink, and was master of the whole construction that Day; But being Desirous to see Brindley resolved to go next Day to Colebrook Dale.'* It is not clear how they took advantage without Mr Broad's knowledge.

The two visitors left twopence for a letter to Mr Broad with a request that he would let the water out of the boiler so that it would be cool enough for them to examine inside on their return. While at Coalbrookdale they were able to see the pieces of a boiler being built by Brindley, but Brindley himself had already left

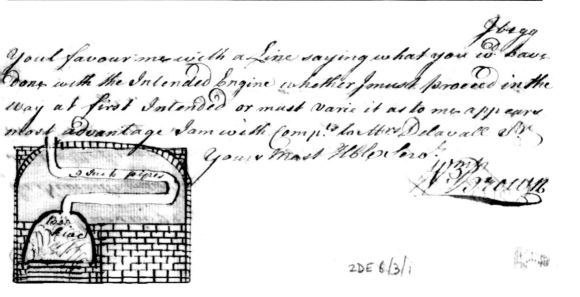

I begg Youl favour me with a Line saying what you wd have done with the Intended Engine whether I must proceed in the way at first Intended or must varie it as to me appears most advantage I am with Compts. (complements) to Mrs Delavall Sr. Your Most Hble Servt. Wm. Brown

William Brown's letter to Mr Delaval was written after viewing Brindley's boiler for an engine (1759). He labelled the 9-inch pipe and 'bee-hive' in his drawing. Note the surrounding brickwork and the iron bars on bricks below the fire.

'*southward*'. They stayed with Abraham Darby for the day as the boiler was being built for him. He '*the master of the great Iron Works there*', was already acquainted with the visitors and showed them everything he knew about it.

However, when they returned to Mr Broad's engine in Fenton, he had gone home, left a letter and shut up the engine still filled with water and fire so that they were unable to see inside. They found it strange that Thomas Broad had said they could see the boiler if Brindley agreed, although Brown's letter confirmed that they had just missed him. The two men from the north thought Broad's attitude '*very bad, nor do we think that he treats Brindley well*'. They would not consider purchasing such an engine without seeing more of it. The long letter was a report to Mr Delaval as he and Lord Ravensworth needed to know if they should invest in the new invention. The Delavals were an important mining family with a seat in Northumberland. Mr Brown suggested checking the contents of Brindley's patent as he thought it more of an improvement than an invention.

Dated 9th September 1759, William Brown's letter from Throckley, Newcastle-upon-Tyne, described Brindley's engine at length. It had four fires on iron bars and bricks, and each fire was under a cast iron '*beehive*' about 3 feet in diameter and height. The fire and flames were directed through the beehive in pipes of nine inches in diameter, and turned this way and that until they reached the chimney at the top. The water was in a boiler formed by a surrounding brick vault, built with '*Extraordinary good bricks*' and the strongest '*Binding lime*' William Brown had ever seen. However, he thought the number of bricks, the cast-iron beehives and the pipes would not be economical for him and the engine house, at a little over 16 feet by 15 feet, was very small. Brindley's chains were of wood, whereas Brown, who had worked with engines since 1750, used lead. Nevertheless, he was interested in using some of Brindley's ideas if they could be adapted to the engine required by Mr Delaval.

There must have been a misunderstanding with Mr Broad as he had written a letter on the 2nd September asking for fair warning of their visit so that he could let out the water and fire. Nearly four months passed by before a letter of 18th December 1759 arrived from Mr Broad explaining that he had not seen James Brindley until the previous night. Mr Broad wrote, *'He* [Brindley] *is engaged in a Navigation Cut in Lancashire, where for some time he cannot be absent on any Account.'* Brindley had directed Mr Broad to write the letter to Mr Delaval and to say that, *'...he is willing to permit you to erect One Engine on his Patent Plan, & leave the gratuity for that Privilege to yr generosity; & if that answers he will agree with you or any other Gentleman on moderate Terms.'* Although Brindley was tied up with the new project of great importance, the letter discloses his generous nature. He offered assistance in constructing the engine and would direct him in the required dimensions if he had the cast metals from Coalbrookdale. Brindley could be found, *'...at Worsley an Estate of the Duke of Bridgewater about Six Miles from Manchester'.*

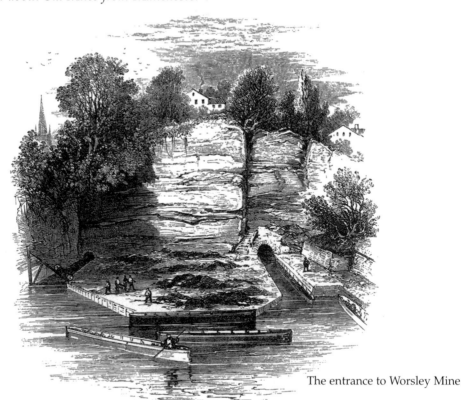

The entrance to Worsley Mine

Brindley and all those involved in the Duke's canal were extremely busy, but Brindley continued to acknowledge those who were still interested in his boiler and the patent. As Smiles commented, *'His was the farthest possible from a narrow or jealous temper, and nothing gave him greater pleasure than to assist others with their inventions...'* Brindley wrote the following letter on 17th March 1764 offering anything to do with

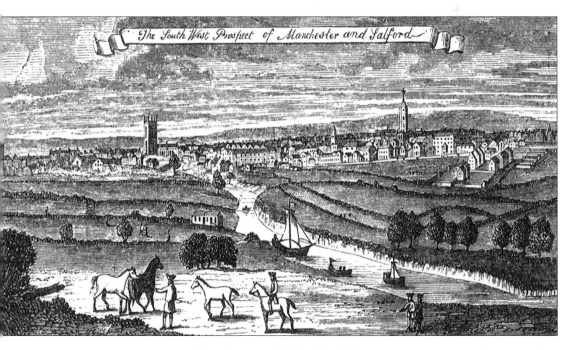

Letter by James Brindley about the boiler (1764)

Manchester and Salford in 1740

the boiler without payment and expressed his willingness to explain it at the *'works'* at Stretford, near Manchester. This rare extant letter was written and signed by James Brindley:

Streatford 17 March 1764

Sir
I recaved your 2 Latters to gather 2: or 3 days be foor this instant as to Consarning my patent aney thing belonging to my Brick Boyler that will be of aney sarvis to you I sall not Expatt ane Reward from you & if you want aney partickler thing Explaining after on part of the Boyler if youl come to our works Il indaver [I'l endeavour] to satisfie you

sr
from yours at Comand

James Brindley

If you wrighe[t] direct to be left at Streatford Turnpike ner Manchester

[The spelling in the above letter gives some indication of Brindley's accent.]

Some years later, James Watt, famed for his advancement of engines, took out a patent with the instruction: *'...working cylinder to be kept as hot as the steam entering it by enclosing it in a case of wood or other slow conductor of heat'*.

By this time James Brindley had been involved with canals for over ten years. His notebook shows that he was introduced to canal work in Staffordshire almost two years before he was working for the Duke of Bridgewater in December 1759. Three of the entries state that he was about the navigation on 5 February 1758 for five days and on 19 February for three days. On another page he wrote neatly, *'Surveing the Nevegation from Long brigg to Kinges Milles or in spected* [sic]', followed by his record of 12¹/₂ days on 18 February 1758 and no further explanation.

Barton Aqueduct over the River Irwell

CHAPTER 3
CANALS AND COLLEAGUES

In 1758, numerous changes were either in embryo or just beginning to emerge. Men of intelligence and influence developed a growing interest in science and enjoyed increasing opportunities for discussing new ideas, discoveries and aids to manufacturing. Knowledge and enterprise increased and the stirrings of the Industrial Revolution were felt in many places. In his later years, James Brindley was acquainted with a group of such men, some of whom belonged to the Lunar Society in Birmingham, an association so called because they met once a month and travelled home by the light of the full moon. In 1758, James Brindley was asked to make a survey for a canal. At the age of forty-two years, he was available just at the right time.

Transport facilities were improved elsewhere by attention to stretches of river, but Staffordshire's rivers rise in the county and continue unsuitable for navigation at its manufacturing towns. The envisaged canal would be independent of rivers and streams. Much talk of this urgent requirement led to James Brindley and his distant family connection, Henry Bradford, making initial surveys in the county. In 1758, Brindley explored what was to become the Staffordshire section of the Trent and Mersey Canal and a stretch between Lichfield and Burton-upon-Trent, while Henry Bradford surveyed the Birmingham to Tamworth line. This researcher believes that the latter route was considered by Henry Bradford junior, who occasionally accompanied his father at Coalbrookdale. His brother Samuel, by then deceased, had been a surveyor and mapmaker of some standing, his work being engraved by Thomas Jeffreys, Geographer to the Prince of Wales. The route to Tamworth passed close to Wigginshill, near Sutton Coldfield, for long the home of the Bradfords and their Quaker Meeting. Earlier in the century, it had been the home of Brindley's great-aunt Esther Bradford (nee Bowman) and for a time of his aunt Esther Ludford (nee Brindley), who was married there in 1714. Hannah, the sister of Henry Bradford, senior, was married to Allen England, of Aldermills at Tamworth, who was described as a *'meat man'*, but he may have been related to a man of the same name who became the manager of the Bridgnorth branch of the Coalbrookdale Company. Who knows what ideas were exchanged at the home and the works of the Darbys?

However, it was the Staffordshire noblemen, including Earl Gower, and the pottery manufacturers who recognised the need and promoted the idea of a Staffordshire canal and there is no proof that Brindley had contact with remote family connections. Early in 1758, James Brindley, by then having the reputation of being 'The Schemer', noted that he had been, *'Surveing the Nevegation from Long brigg to Kinges Milles or in spected'*. Longbridge was near Burslem and King's Mills lay beyond Burton-upon-Trent. It was Brindley's first long distance survey, but the work involved rather more than riding his patient mare along a suitable and level course of over forty-five miles. A photograph of Brindley's 1758 estimate for a navigation between Lichfield and Burton-upon-Trent shows that he measured the fall of water

| The Duke of Bridgewater as a young man | Extract from Brindley's pocket-book |

from pools, suggested the sites of bridges [aqueducts], fords, and fences, noted the position of mills and considered the purchase of land. Such detail must have required Brindley's concentrated attention. He had not seen such a canal and yet the estimate bears the date one year before he began the experience of a major construction with the Duke of Bridgewater and John Gilbert. On 1 December 1759, a printed leaflet described the Lichfield to Burton survey as the work of Mr James Brindley *'and other skilful persons'*, but there is nothing to indicate when the latter were called in. Brindley's notebook is as brief as ever for this period and his entries for 1758 do not refer to Lichfield or Burton-upon-Trent.

In the mid-18th century, the transport of commodities was very difficult. The condition of most roads only allowed packhorses and a few carts through the rutted tracks, while bad weather caused towns to be cut off and inhabitants to become short of supplies. Manchester was such a town, with a population of a few thousand. The people needed cheap coal, but the young Duke of Bridgewater's collieries could only transport it on the backs of packhorses or by cart to the River Irwell. It was carried for a few miles on the river boats and then transferred again for carriage to the town by horses or carts, thus increasing inconvenience and costs.

The Duke's father had planned improvements but did not proceed with them. The new Duke's agent, John Gilbert, prepared fresh plans during 1758 and applied to Parliament for an Act to be passed early in the following year. The idea was to build a canal from Worsley and halve the cost of coal in Manchester. Although the Duke had seen the French Languedoc Canal on a visit to Europe, he must have known that tradesmen and manufacturers in other parts of England were also talking of canals and the linking of rivers, as Earl Gower, of Trentham in North Staffordshire, was his brother-in-law.

In July 1759, Brindley was called northwards to consider the project of the Duke and his agent, who required his assistance at Worsley. The Duke may have heard of Brindley from several sources, for Brindley had acquired a degree of expertise which convinced the Duke that he was the man for the job. The successful Wet Earth Colliery scheme was only three miles from Worsley, involved the same river and had given Brindley experience in channelling water underground, tunnelling, brickwork, the construction of an underground chamber and the direction of labour on an untried plan. Brindley's millwork had provided years of practice in controlling water on minor rivers and streams, and observed improved river channels. He was able to envisage the requirements to make the Staffordshire survey for Earl Gower. In addition, James's brother, Joseph, was a millwright in the vicinity of John Gilbert's native village of Alton, where Thomas Gilbert, the brother of John, was to sub-let the Alton Smelting Mill to Joseph Brindley. The mill was the property of the Earl of Shrewsbury and situated in Dimmingsdale, close to the confluence with the River Churnet. The two eldest Brindley brothers were familiar with the same river and during the 1760s James, Joseph and John Brindley were well known to the Gilberts.

In 1759 Francis Egerton, the Duke of Bridgewater, at twenty-three years of age, was the youngest of the group called 'The Triumvirate' by Wedgwood. The nobleman, his thirty-five year old agent and James Brindley, already aged forty-three years, were seemingly from very different backgrounds and yet had some elements in common. The Duke's education had been neglected by his mother, who thought him dull, but at the age of twelve he succeeded to the title unexpectedly and was sent to school. Later, he made the customary Grand Tour of Europe with a tutor. John Gilbert had attended the small village school near his home at Alton and settled in an apprenticeship with a Birmingham buckle-maker named Matthew Boulton. Boulton's son and namesake became famous for fine metal work and for his partnership with James Watt in the manufacture of steam engines. Unfortunately, John Gilbert's training was incomplete when he was called to return to Alton on the death of his father. He gained experience in managing the family property, with interests in the limestone quarries at nearby Cauldon and mining elsewhere in the district. His elder brother, Thomas Gilbert, trained as a lawyer and became the agent, or steward, for Earl Gower and the Bridgewater estates, while John held the post as agent at Worsley. James Brindley's education was said to have been neglected by his father, but James had completed his seven-year apprenticeship and followed it with twenty years of business and technical experience in a self-employed capacity, maintaining two premises and assistants.

At this time the Duke and Brindley were both bachelors, free to devote all their time and energy to the canal project. The equally hard working John Gilbert had a family and attended to the canal plans, the construction, the hire of labour, the management of the estate and the Duke's constant financial struggle for his ambitious scheme. The Duke was not living in luxury at Worsley, for he reduced his spending to the minimum in his effort to save for the canal. Smiles tells how the Duke was out in all weathers and even mistaken for a labourer in his own coal-yard when asked to assist a customer by lifting a full sack onto the back of a poor man. Nowadays, the three at the construction would be called workaholics and wear protective clothing against weather and accident, but *Rees's Cyclopaedia* and Dr Aikin, a theology tutor at Warrington Academy, saw fit to include a comment on the appearance and manner of Brindley as a *'mere peasant ...no better than one of his own carters'*. Brindley was brought up to do farm work, for which it is normal to wear old clothes, and his Quaker relatives would have dressed 'plain', in their own simple style. Brindley knew how to rise to the occasion though and went shopping in London, when he and Gilbert presented plans at the meeting of the House of Commons Committee. Brindley's notebook shows that he purchased shoes, breeches, a coat and a waistcoat of broadcloth, spent one shilling on being shaved four times and sixpence having his shoes blacked, until there was *'left in my pokite £1 12s 6d'*.

The Duke of Bridgewater used the speech of the Worsley area, while Gilbert and Brindley, being from neighbouring districts of Staffordshire, most likely had some similarities of accent and dialect. These personal details can only be imagined. However, Dr Aikin quoted from a letter in which Brindley was described as *'unlettered and rude of speech'*. This led to descriptions such as that in the *Encyclopaedia Britannica* (1947), *'Brindley retained to the last a peculiar roughness of character and demeanor'*. A Rees's, or his contributor's, impression of Brindley's language was, *'...mean, obscure and almost unintelligible'*, but he continued with the following view: *'His countenance was sensible and animated ...his conversation, on occasions of importance and among his intimate friends, was instructive and interesting'*. In time, Brindley's friend, Josiah Wedgwood, who knew and respected him better than anyone, was able to write, *'I always edify as much in that man's company as at Church I promise myself to be much wiser the following'*, and even Aikin acknowledged that all ears listened when Brindley spoke.

Although the original Bridgewater Canal and Worsley Mine plans had been passed before Brindley was called upon, they were altered. This necessitated further visits to the House of Commons Committee, where Brindley gave convincing demonstrations and answered questions. Gilbert and Brindley presented ideas that were new to the members, who were naturally concerned that the canal would leak. Brindley persuaded them that the seal would hold by demonstrating 'puddling' on the floor of the Chamber with a mixture of clay, sand and water, worked to such a consistency that it could not absorb more water. This created a seal. The use of clay as a sealant had been known for thousands of years and, nowadays archaeologists discover clay linings at the base of Roman bath-houses. Brindley was said to have assisted demonstrations by modelling in cheese, the cheapest medium. On one visit to London, Brindley purchased a knife and made a note of it in his pocket-book.

While in the capital, John Gilbert and his wife took James Brindley to see a performance of Richard III by the actor David Garrick, who had spent his boyhood in Lichfield, but Brindley was upset and vowed that he would never go to the theatre again. Such a Shakespearean play may have been unsuitable for a first attendance and the choice of something lighter might have been preferable, but Brindley was probably too much of a workaholic to be impressed and interested in theatre.

With little written material readily available and Brindley's notebooks being brief and scarce, there can be differing opinions as to who was responsible for specific constructions in the Duke's project. John Phillips, who had worked with Brindley, was prepared to quote Richard Whitworth, Esq, in '...*admiring the wonderful and great natural genius, of Mr James Brindley, who planned the same, and perfected these canals*'. Rees's publication included separate tributes to John Gilbert and James Brindley, declaring that Gilbert had worked out the canal scheme in the Bull Inn in Manchester. '*Mr Gilbert's name had seldom occurred in connection with this very important and lucrative undertaking, and as he preceded Mr Brindley in this business of which we have ample evidence, we thought that justice required a candid and impartial statement of the case*', and that, '*Mr G.' was probably so modest and unassuming, that he did not, during his lifetime, lay claim to the honour which belonged to him, with respect to the Duke of Bridgewater's canals and collieries; and we have introduced his name ...to do him justice, without meaning to detract from the merit of his coadjutor and successor, Mr Brindley, to whom we have already paid ample and deserved respect*'. Earlier, the account claimed, '*the tunnel was entirely executed, as well as planned by Mr G, who being acquainted with Mr Brindley as a neighbour, and knowing him to be a very ingenious and excellent millwright, engaged his assistance*'.

Of course, the Duke, Gilbert and Brindley had disagreements at times, for they were all determined men with forward looking ideas and yet they were totally dependent upon each other for success. Temporary discord evaporated, for their cooperation was essential and their experience was complementary. Gilbert had been engaged in family business, mining and quarrying, while Brindley could contribute his working knowledge of tunnelling, the creation of an underground chamber, management of surplus water and the invention of simple engines. Two hundred years later, F Mullineux thought that it was impossible to say which of the two men devised the scheme at Worsley, where the canal reached into the mine, made use of a basin for boats and was at the beginning of extensive tunnelling, which continued long after Brindley had left. In 1961, the Duke of Bridgewater, John Gilbert and James Brindley were honoured with a plaque at the entrance to the system. The three had spent many evenings close by, discussing plans and financial problems, either at an inn or in the Hall at Worsley, where Brindley was provided with accommodation.

Rees did not refer to the engine used at Worsley for the removal of water from the mining area, but a letter of 30 September 1763 from Manchester, claimed that, '*Many gentlemen of this neighbourhood are reaping the benefit of Mr Brindley's invention, he having taught them a method of draining coal pits by a fire engine, constructed at the expense of 150 l. [£150], which no one before knew how to make at less than 500 l' [£500] (History of Inland Navigations*, 2nd edit.). Brindley had used wooden chains and a cylinder of deal instead of cast iron, having gained his experience as early as 1756. On the other hand, John Gilbert was to declare later, in his own handwriting, that he himself knew nothing of engines and his letter to Matthew Boulton of Birmingham gives a unique insight into Gilbert's apprehension.

Seven years after Brindley's death, John Gilbert was dependent on the advice of the famous manufacturers of engines, Matthew Boulton and James Watt. By then the Gilbert brothers were in business with Earl Gower at Donnington Wood Colliery, Shropshire, for which they had purchased a Boulton & Watt engine and it seems appropriate to quote part of the letter dated 23 April 1779:

'...there is a Steam Case to the Cillender ...I think I had requested Mr Hall not to Order one without your or Mr Watses particular directions I shud have been happy to have seen you or Mr Wats upon the place but its too late now ...Exchanging Engineres is not all ways an advantage to a Consern Mr Hall ...would do all in his power to get us the Castings at Both places well done and as right as was prudent and as our people was not much acquainted with the Engine ffurnies [Furnace] *beg'd he would look particularly to every point that everything moved properly together I wish I had seen you and Mr Hornblower together when he first came to us that all things might have been well consider'd ...as I wish our people to attend particularly to the directions of the person you appoint ...as I am an entire stranger to Engine Work must beg the ffavour of you or Mr Wats to look over the Bills of all the Castings and materials and settle them for us'.*

At the foot of the letter, Gilbert wrote, *'I doubt not there is particulars go with all the materials from Birmingham that are for the Engine so that they may be seen they are right when they arrive there'.* John Gilbert's use of an old style without punctuation and clarification demands more than one reading, but he did not sound at all confident about the new engine. He had a tendency to add afterthoughts to his message.

The famous James Watt answered the rather anxious letter in Matthew Boulton's absence on 29 April 1779 with, *'I fancy you mistake the heating case for what we used to call an outside cylinder which cost double the money the heating case does being much heavier and of much greater price per ton'.* Regarding the change of engineer, Watt explained that Mr Hall was inexperienced and they had *'brought Mr Hornblower from Cornwall for Donnington Wood and I do assure you he is the best putter together of an engine, I ever saw'* and *'as Mr Hall had very injudiciously planned several things about the Engine house I was obliged to order them to be altered and to me and to Mr Hornblower you are to attribute these alterations ...as I don't know that he has done anything without consulting me'.*

By 20 October 1779, Matthew Boulton, known to Gilbert since boyhood, was obliged to write to him beginning, *'I intended not to trouble you upon the subject of payment for Donnington Engine till Xmas but I am disappointed of a very large sum viz £4000 which I expected on 29 Sept.'* Boulton postponed this payment until Lady Day (25 March) and added, *'...there is nothing charged in our bill for work higher than common prices and upon the whole of it I am sure we don't gain one farthing perhaps you may ask why I have added 20 guineas to which I counter, ... when you have paid £300* [£10,000 now?] *I shall give you a licence and a receipt.'*

There was no apparent ill feeling and Gilbert continued his involvement with Boulton and Watt for the rest of his life. He may have had temporary problems with his many businesses, or he may have delayed payment until the last moment in the manner of some modern businessmen. However, this episode may throw some light on a letter quoted in Smiles' book, in which Brindley's widow referred to *'repeated applications'* she had made to Gilbert regarding money owed to her late husband for the period 1765-1772. Without full accounts it is unwise to comment, but Ann had received *'constant promises'* and £100 handed to her brother by John Gilbert in 1774. Debts for the canal construction had been considerable, but with burgeoning trade the Duke began to make a fortune and eventually bought works of art. Even in 1765 he was able to order a cream dinner service from Josiah Wedgwood. Brindley's widow made another unsuccessful claim in 1803, the year of the Duke's death. Smiles described how the 'Triumvirate' sat discussing financial problems when the Duke asked, *'Well, Brindley, what's to be done now? How are we to get at money for finishing the canal?'* to which Brindley replied, *'Well, Duke I can't tell, I only know that if the money can be got, I can finish the canal, and it will pay well.'* It was John Gilbert who had the difficult task of collecting enough to pay the wages.

Although John Gilbert had talent in what was to become known as civil engineering, the letter from Matthew Boulton revealed another aspect, for Boulton had *'doubts about the management'* of the Donnington Wood engine and that, *'You have no man of knowledge sufficient whenever you are of the same opinion (which I hope will not be produced by woeful experience) I shall send you the best man I happen to have in my power.'* Assistants reported to Boulton that the boiler was leaking *'much'* and the cylinder and steam pipe were not airtight and should be rectified. Boulton also warned John Gilbert against exceeding the capacity of the engine.

On 27 February 1789, the firm of Boulton and Watt produced a technical drawing for part of an engine for Gilbert's rock salt mine at Marston, in Cheshire, but Gilbert's letter concerning the technicalities was not written by him or by his son, and he added a paragraph expressing a wish to meet Boulton and Watt's representative at The Crown in Stone. The letter shows John Gilbert was still willing to learn, even at sixty-five years of age, but he missed the meeting, *'...which prevents me knowing so much about the Engine as I ought to have done'*, and the drawing had to be returned to Boulton and Watt *'in a clean condition'*. On 4 June 1791, four years before Gilbert's death, his son, also named John, wrote to Matthew Boulton with a rather surprising request, for he asked Boulton if he could recommend a surveyor for a canal in Manchester, as *'you know people of abilities'*.

The letters show unfamiliarity with words such as engineer, cylinder and furnace, but few dictionaries were available or used as nowadays. Mistakes in common words and the absence of punctuation were not unusual. Smiles mentioned that the Duke wrote little and preferred to conduct business in person, so the trusted Gilbert was the only one of the three likely to write anything which might be called a record. James Brindley was employed when required by the Duke, but John Gilbert remained as the Duke's agent for the rest of his life, continued to live at Worsley, ran his own businesses and purchased the Clough Hall estate at Kidsgrove, near the Goldenhill Collieries, in North Staffordshire.

Eventually, long after Brindley had gone, the tunnelling at the Worsley mine extended to a considerable mileage on several planes, but the initial development benefited from his ideas and introductions concerning the water, the pumps, the engine and the ventilation, at least. Unfortunately there is no written record. Rees's volume has most of the Memoir of Brindley including, *'...envy and prejudice and an attachment to established customs, raised a variety of obstacles to the accomplishment of his design and undertakings; and if he had not been liberally and powerfully protected by the Duke of Bridgewater, at the commencement of the business, his triumph over the opposition with which he encountered must have been in a very considerable degree obstructed and retarded. ...Mr Brindley ...persevered ...Having completed the canal as far as Barton ...he prepared to carry it over that river, by an aquaeduct'.*

Rees's short biography of John Gilbert does not mention the Barton Aqueduct, yet there was the opportunity to record Gilbert's part, for he and his men certainly worked on the structure, which carried the canal on arches over the River Irwell. Accounts for two hundred years have implied that it was Brindley with the *'absolutely impracticable'* ideas resulting in the Duke's requirement of a second opinion of the proposed aqueduct, and it is believed to have been John Smeaton, engineer, who made the now famous remark, *'I have often heard of Castles in the air; but never before saw where any of them were to be erected'.* Consequently, when Smeaton was employed on the Forth and Clyde Canal in 1768 Brindley was required to give an opinion, as he was often asked to do. Smeaton seemed as exasperated by Brindley as on their first encounter and was unable to resist a jibe at Brindley's proposals and success with aqueducts, they being his *'hobby horse'.*

Phillips described the Barton Aqueduct as being of great strength and thickness, *'... every front stone has five square faces or beds, well jointed and cramped with iron run in with lead ...the piers, are of the largest blocks of stone and crampt as before'.* The structure was 200 yards long, 12 yards wide and 39 feet above the river, with supporting embankments at both ends. The central arch of the three spanned 63 feet and Brindley included underwater gates to section off the aqueduct as a precaution against accident. This section was filled with water as a group of important people watched and waited. The process seemed to go well, but Smiles related how small cracks appeared in one of the arches, which had to be rectified immediately by John Gilbert and his men with straw and more *'puddling'.* Brindley, naturally overcome with anxiety, retired to his bed at a Stretford inn. Nevertheless, the structure was stable enough to be in use until its demolition in 1894, when it was replaced by the Manchester Ship Canal. From its opening on 17 July 1761, boats pulled by one mule were seen moving slowly over the aqueduct, while several men hauled boats upstream on the river below. By 1765, the structure was described as, *'...perhaps the greatest curiosity in the world ...crowds of people, including those of the first fashion, resort to it daily'.*

The view of one spectator is recorded in the *History of Inland Navigations*: *'Whilst I was surveying it was a mixture of wonder and delight; four barges passed me in the space of about three minutes, two of them being chained together, and dragged by two horses, who went on the terras of the canal, whereon, I must own, I durst hardly venture to walk, as I almost trembled to behold the large river Irwell underneath me, across which this navigation is carried by a bridge, which contains upon it the canal of water, with barges in it, drawn by horses, which walk upon the battlements of this extraordinary bridge.'*

Although the purpose of the Duke's canal was to transport coal and other commodities, he soon found enough pleasure in it to have his own gondola and took guests on canal trips. The Duke had invited important people to the opening of the aqueduct and, within a few years, he had devised a scheme for visitors to the mine at Worsley. A letter *'to a Lady'* explains that names could be sent to the Duke's new house and tickets obtained to enter the underground system to see the *'curiosity'*: *'You enter with lighted candles the subterraneous passage in a boat, made for bringing out coals, of this form and dimension. Fifty feet long, four and a half broad. Two feet three inches deep. When you first enter the passage and again when you come among the colliers, your heart will be apt to fail you: for it seems so much like leaving this world for the regions of darkness, ...should your spirits sink, the company are ever ready to aid you with a glass of wine... Through this passage you proceed towing the boat on each hand by a rail, to the extent of a thousand yards.'* The entrance was only six feet wide, but it opened further inside so that boats could pass, and by this time there were vertical ventilation shafts reaching 37 yards high. This particular visitor already foresaw how his accustomed leisure could continue as, *'...if the boats were covered we might travel by night or by day, and sleep, read, write, play cards, drink tea, and partake of a thousand diversions.'*

It is difficult to imagine Brindley taking such a trip, but Josiah Wedgwood, who was often at Earl Gower's Trentham home in a business and social capacity, spent eight hours in the company of the Duke of Bridgewater at Worsley and was then taken for a ride of nine miles along the canal. Accompanied by Mr Sparrow, the solicitor, Wedgwood enjoyed travelling over Barton Aqueduct in the Duke's vessel. He wrote to Dr Erasmus Darwin on 10 July 1765 to say that it had been drawn by a mule for one and a half hours, *'...along the most delightful valley, at least it appeared so to me'*. It was said that the Duke spoke of little else but canals. If Brindley's status and contribution to the Bridgewater project was exaggerated, a modern suggestion, then the Duke and the Earl had ample opportunity to set the record straight. The clever Josiah Wedgwood and Dr Darwin had faith in Brindley's ability and respect for his honesty. They were outward-looking men who associated with members of the Lunar Society in Birmingham and others from further afield. They would have understood Brindley's position.

Phillips described Brindley's control of water at the Castlefield end of the Duke's canal. On the River Medlock he built, *'...a large and beautiful wear [weir] comprised of six segments of a circle, built of squared stone and bedded in terras, every stone crampt with iron and flushed in with melted lead ...with a circular nave of stone in the middle'*, which took the overflow of surplus water under the navigation and down to the river at a point downstream. Excess water turned a waterwheel of thirty feet in diameter so that a hoist could lift coal through a shaft to where it was loaded on the hill. Brindley had built a weir, shafts and a waterwheel of a large diameter for the project at Wet Earth Colliery, albeit for a different purpose. The invention of the hoist at Castlefield, the ventilation system at Worsley, a machine *'for sifting sand and mixing mortar'* and other contrivances were attributed to Brindley.

Following his involvement with the Duke of Bridgewater during the early 1760s, Brindley was busy on his own account and the period included his 1763 visit to Coalbrookdale when the Walker Colliery engine was being built. The Duke had by no means finished his canal and his famous project continued for seventeen years.

Brindley was again involved when this first canal independent of a river was required to cross difficult bogland called Sale Moor, towards Runcorn, in Cheshire. The undertaking proved to be a mammoth task needing drainage and the building of embankments of deal balks, oak piles, earth and clay, to be rammed without the aid of modern equipment. Brindley was at Sale Moor in 1765, and in that year he had meetings with Josiah Wedgwood, who had been promoting the Staffordshire Canal with great enthusiasm. Of course, a possible route across Cheshire and the progress of the Duke of Bridgewater's canal towards Liverpool were under consideration. Wedgwood and the solicitor had presented plans to the Duke on their visit to Worsley early in July 1765. There were meetings, discussions, alternative routes, disagreements, rivalries and much to-ing and fro-ing between important people with differing interests, but Wedgwood's letters to his friends and family provide a record of his involvement as a leading promoter and of his contact with James Brindley. On 2 January of the same year, there was a disagreement which took John and Josiah Wedgwood, John Sparrow, the solicitor, and James Brindley thirty miles southward: '...*promoting our GENERAL CAUSE, we altogether posted away to Lichfield'*. Thomas Gilbert and Samuel Garbett had arrived, followed by Lord Gower, and, although Wedgwood's party was not expected, *'We were called to sup with Lord Gower in the midst of our debates'*. By now, James Brindley was accustomed to meeting people from all walks of life in heated discussion.

On 11 March, Wedgwood wrote to his brother that he and Brindley had dined together before a meeting at The Leopard, an inn which still flourishes in the centre of Burslem. Discussion of the navigation continued at a further meeting in Hanley, the next day. On 4 May 1765, Wedgwood had informed Dr Darwin that Brindley was coming especially from Lancashire for a meeting, which took place at Newcastle-under-Lyme on 13 May and, '...*when Brindley comes over I shall be able to send you a long string of facts'*. It was a busy time of preparation and on 10 July 1765 Wedgwood was under pressure of work. He wrote many letters, including one to Dr Darwin, to whom he gave thanks for the instructions respecting the Rivers Soar and Idle, which are tributaries of the Trent in its lower navigable section. Waterways other than those of Staffordshire were taken into consideration. Dr Darwin was thanked for his *'ingenious design for the map'*, although the subject was not disclosed. The letter continued, *'I have wrote about a yard square to Mr Brindley last week and this morning to which I hope to have an answer this week & shall transmitt the contents to you'*. Wedgwood proceeded with a description of his trip in the Duke of Bridgewater's gondola during his visit to Worsley, where he had presented the plans for the navigation to the Duke. In addition to promoting canals, Wedgwood had to attend to experiments and designs in clay, the management of his pottery and the gaining of profitable orders from far and wide. The letter to Dr Darwin shows that he became a little fanciful after his commercial success in obtaining an order for a tea and coffee set to be made for Queen Charlotte, the wife of George III. Wedgwood had been to London to see the Queen and on his return wrote, *'Her Majesty was pleased at the time she gave this order to signify her royal intention of encouraging the British manufacturers all in her power ... Is not this encouragement for dedicating our grand design of uniteing the two seas, to a Patriot*

Queen who thus knows how to extend her benign influence to the remotest & meanest of her subjects?' In the preceding paragraph Wedgwood told Darwin, *'...but I have the honour to be employed by the intended Patroness of the River Charlotte...'* The idea of the canal system being named the River Charlotte after the Queen does not seem to have been repeated and with Brindley's view that rivers were only to feed canals, it was unlikely that he would have been agreeable to the suggestion.

MAP OF 93 MILES OF THE TRENT AND MERSEY CANAL

During the summer months of 1765, the chief concern was to obtain an agreement on the route of the Staffordshire Canal, or Grand Trunk, across Cheshire towards Liverpool and to determine whether the Duke of Bridgewater would or would not agree to a connection with his still incomplete waterway. Eventually, the extended waterway became the Trent and Mersey Canal. Following a meeting with John Gilbert, Wedgwood had concluded that the Duke was a steady friend in the matter and an order was made at the Newcastle meeting that Mr Hugh Henshall, with assistance, should plan a level route across Cheshire between Harecastle and the Duke's navigation. Landowners along the suggested routes were difficult to handle and there was a time when Josiah Wedgwood could not be sure which side Earl Gower was taking.

In the midst of all this pressure James Brindley was married at St Margaret's Church, Wolstanton, to the teenaged Ann Henshall, sister to the above mentioned Hugh Henshall and the daughter of John Henshall, a surveyor known to Brindley for some years. The marriage, which took place by licence on 8 December 1765, may have been 'arranged' as was often the case in those days, and Brindley, now called an *'engineer'* on his marriage bond, probably spent little time with his bride. Soon after 13 December, Wedgwood wrote to Thomas Bentley, *'I have seen Mr Brindley again & told him that our present situation oblig'd me to put a few serious & very important questions to him, that I consider'd his connection with the D [Duke] & did not desire him to do anything inconsistant with them, but that a whole Country depended upon his well known abilities & integrity to prevent their being deceived in such important points from any quarter'.*

By 30 December, an agreement was reached and the meeting at Wolseley Bridge, near Stafford, was the most important that had yet taken place. Earl Gower was the chairman of the meeting, which was attended by Lord Grey (later Earl of Stamford), three MPs and *'many others of local weight and influence'*, including Wedgwood, Bentley and Brindley. Wedgwood spoke *'with effect'* and Brindley, according to Meteyard, writing one hundred years after the event, was called upon to state his plans, which he brought forward with such *'extraordinary lucidity of detail as to make them clear to the dullest intellect present'*. Although it is often said that Brindley worked without plans, he was able to recommend a Mr Oldham of Manchester for the making of a new plate for printing the map. Wedgwood promptly made arrangements to meet the gentleman. There was still a great deal to be done; other schemes were planned and rivalry added to the pressure to see the Acts through Parliament, whereas Brindley's advice was sought for several projects running at the same time.

Meteyard described Brindley's examination at the House of Commons, when members of the old navigation *'received their death blow'*. 'Of course the opposing counsel *'pooh pooh'd as usual, made small puns about 'air castles', and were ridiculously incorrect in many assertions, particularly as to the feasibility of an aqueduct across the swampy land about the Dane; but the great engineer pointed to the triumphs he had already achieved with the Duke's canal, and asserted that his proposal to carry the Trent and Mersey canal by a tunnel through the high ground of Harecastle, was one which, however difficult, he could accomplish'*. When difficulties arose, some thought such confidence had been unwise. The idea was to use the surplus water from local coalmines and reduce the number of locks required.

Thomas Bentley wrote a promotional pamphlet in which he referred to *'various experiments'* made by the Duke of Bridgewater and, with this experience, Brindley made his estimate for the Trent and Mersey Canal. The sum of £700 per mile would cover the purchase of land and the construction of locks, towing paths and bridges between Wilden Ferry, in Derbyshire, and Harecastle, at the Staffordshire/Cheshire border, while the cost of cutting the canal would be £1,000 per mile, with a *'supposed'* £10,000 required for the penetration of Harecastle. The canal was to be twelve feet wide at the bottom and usually three feet deep. Boats able to carry loads of 20 tons were to be 70 feet long and 6 feet wide, with detachable rudders for use at either end so that the vessels did not require turning. Each £30 boat was to be worked by one man and a boy, and drawn by a horse capable of pulling three boats at a time, when necessary.

Mr Samuel Garbett of Birmingham wrote that measurements between Wilden Ferry and Stone were *'under the Inspection of Mr Smeaton, FRS & Mr Brindley, the Duke of Bridgewater's Principal Engineer'*. The total length of the canal to Runcorn was 93 miles and required 6 tunnels, 91 locks and 127 aqueducts and culverts. Brindley called the Trent and Mersey Canal the Grand Trunk, because of the envisaged branches, and the Acts of Parliament for it and its first branch were passed on the same day in 1766. By linking the Rivers Trent, Mersey and Severn with the Trent and Mersey Canal and the branch Staffordshire and Worcestershire Canal, there would be navigation between Liverpool, Hull and Bristol. The Staffordshire and Worcestershire Canal records are now preserved on many reels of film and date from the beginning of the history of that waterway in the spring of 1766 when, *'James Brindley of Worsley in the County of Lancaster Engineer, was elected surveyor ...A Surveyor (at £200 per annum) who is to level and set out the several works superintend and inspect the Execution of them',* while Mr James Baker, the Clerk of the Works was *'to see everything carried out at the Surveyor's instructions'.*

The meeting concerning the Trent and Mersey Canal took place at The Crown in Stone on 10 June 1766, when James Brindley was appointed Surveyor General, at a salary of £200 per annum, Hugh Henshall, his brother-in-law, became *'The Clerk of the Works'* at £150 per annum and Josiah Wedgwood elected to be the Treasurer without a salary. Wedgwood and other potters, along with interested noblemen, were the chief supporters and shareholders as materials for manufacturing were required, and finished pottery goods needed reliable carriage with fewer breakages. The steady glide of the canal boat would be ideal.

Stone in 1830

On 26 July 1766, Josiah Wedgwood cut the first turf at Brownhills, just to the north of Longbridge, where the canalside port for Burslem was to develop and become known as Longport. James Brindley wheeled the turf away and the rejoicing continued as notable people were given the honour of digging and removing turves in a wheelbarrow. Most likely James's brother, John, was one of them as he was a potter with shares in the canal. Poorer folk enjoyed a bonfire in front of Josiah Wedgwood's house and a sheep was roasted in Burslem marketplace.

The work began at Wilden Ferry, where there were few problems, and at Harecastle, where the tunnel was to be Brindley's challenge, the rock being so hard that it took eleven years of dangerous toil to finish the 2,880 yard tunnel. During the next century, its dimensions of nine feet wide and twelve feet high proved to be inadequate and Thomas Telford substituted a second tunnel which ran alongside Brindley's original. Due to the hardness of the rock Telford found the work almost as difficult. Brindley's tunnel could only take a narrow boat and the boatmen had to 'leg it' through by lying on their backs and 'walking' their feet along the sides of the tunnel, whereas Telford's construction was wide enough to take a towpath so that the towing horse was able to continue to haul the boat for more than $1^1/2$ miles underground. Brindley died five years before the Trent and Mersey Canal was completed, but he ensured that his 38 year-old brother-in-law, Hugh Henshall, was well prepared to take over as surveyor and bring the undertaking to a conclusion in 1777.

The work at Harecastle proceeded from both ends and at intervals along the route, where shafts had been sunk for ventilation and the removal of waste. Brindley arranged pumps operated by watermills and windmills until his simple engine was installed. Descriptions are limited to the often repeated impressions of a bystander, a gentleman from Burslem who, in September 1767, wrote the now famous lines:

'Gentlemen come to view our eighth wonder of the world, the subterraneous navigation, which is cutting by the great Mr Brindley, who handles rocks as easily as you would plum pies, and makes the four elements subservient to his will... all ears listen, and every mind is filled with wonder at the things he pronounces to be practicable. He has cut a mile through bogs, which he binds up, embanking them with stone which he gets out of other parts of the navigation, besides about a quarter of a mile into the hill Yelden, on the other side of which he has a pump worked by water, and a stove, the fire of which sucks through a pipe the damps that would annoy the men who are cutting towards the centre of the hill. The clay he cuts out served for bricks to arch the subterranean part ....'

Where necessary, bricks line the tunnels at Wet Earth Colliery, Worsley and Harecastle, and once more Brindley's economical steam engine was employed to remove copious amounts of water. Such water was eventually required to supply the canal at this high place, the summit of its route across the plain of Cheshire and the Trent valley of Staffordshire.

Brindley was said to have planned a branch tunnel to a mine at Goldenhill, where land and premises at Oldcott, Goldenhill and Turnhurst had been purchased on 22 May 1760 for £2300 by Robert Hurst of Cheadle, Staffordshire. Hurst was a relation of the Gilberts and the sites included sources of coal, limestone and ironstone, not far from the Henshalls' home at Newchapel. Tenants occupied the properties, one being John Taylor, an earth potter, who held several buildings and lands, including a house, workplace and pot oven at Goldenhill. On 24 September 1760, four months after Hurst's transaction, John Brindley married a widow whose maiden name had been Taylor. Perhaps this was a coincidence, but in 1808 John Brindley bequeathed his Goldenhill property to Thomas John Brindley, a grandson.

These events of 1760 took place long before the Duke's first canal was complete, but deeds dating from the beginning of December 1772 list the holders of shares in the above properties. The date has significance as James Brindley had died on 27 September 1772 and Hugh Henshall completed the administration of Brindley's estate for probate on 18 December 1772. Just sixteen days earlier, on 2 December, Hugh Henshall paid £1000 to Robert Hurst for an undivided fourth of the estate purchased by Hurst in 1760, but no reference was made to James Brindley's recent death. Previously, the undivided fourths had been arranged thus: one for the benefit of Thomas Gilbert and John Gilbert, one for William Bate and John Brindley, one for James Brindley, and the remaining fourth for Robert Hurst and his heirs. A schedule of 1818 showed that Robert Williamson, the second husband of James Brindley's widow, was soon brought into the partnership from 1775. Strangely, a claim by the widowed daughter-in-law of John Gilbert failed through lack of evidence of a conveyance to the Gilberts. Smiles stated that James Brindley had paid £543 6s 8d for his share, although Smiles believed that the sum, or part of it, had been borrowed from Mr Lancelot of Leek.

The first twenty-two miles of the Trent and Mersey Canal were completed in two years. A considerable distance was expected to be navigable in a further eighteen months time, but the work at Harecastle delayed completion of the whole. There were those who thought that Brindley was wasting money on such tunnelling, but Telford's replacement tunnel took the same route. The North Staffordshire Railway Company took their line from Stoke to Crewe through the rock and opened it in 1848. On nationalisation, in 1948, the newly-formed British Rail took over the line from the LMS (London, Midland, and Scottish). Steam engines were phased out and the new electrified route by-passes Harecastle on the western side, using a short section of the old route at the approach to Kidsgrove.

Other tunnels, locks and aqueducts were built, for the canal passed over the River Trent several times as well as the Rivers Dane and Dove. The latter was crossed near to Burton-upon-Trent with a fine aqueduct of twenty-three arches covering a distance of $1^1/4$ miles. At Alrewas is the strange sight of a level crossing of the canal with the River Trent. Surplus water goes over a weir and continues as the river. Piles were driven into the river bed to support a footbridge. The towing horse had to guide the boat through the river and into the canal, a procedure which could be hazardous when the river was full. At Rugeley an aqueduct crossed the Trent at Brindley's Bank and was said to have, '...*withstood the floods of the river for more than half a century without requiring material repairs*'. The 1840 tithe map shows a gravel pit occupied by the Canal company in the vicinity of the aqueduct, while the 1760 map of Brindley's Staffordshire survey, revised by John Smeaton, carried a list of landowners whose land, '...*through which it is proposed to pass*'. Heading the list are Mr Brindley and his friend John Shrigley, with 18 chains 20 links [606 yards 2 feet], presumably in North Staffordshire as the plan works down the Trent valley. Another plot of 220 yards at Rugeley was in the name of Mr Brindley only. If the names of the landowners were noted in 1760, Brindley was in possession of these plots at a very early stage, but they may have been added to the map nearer to the time of construction, when he would have seen the advantage of having a gravel pit near to the aqueduct at Rugeley.

Brindley maintained his principal method of following a contour level as far as possible, so that Simeon Shaw, writing in 1829, commented on the Trent and Mersey Canal at Stoke where, '*The Canal passes over the Trent at this place, the Acqueduct* [sic] *being of three brick arches; and so very level with the adjoining land, as rarely to be noticed by persons passing along that way*'.

and *their* Heirs forever, *the* annual Rent or Sum of *Money*, *herein before stipulated* ————————

by two equal Half-Yearly Payments. Viz: on every *twenty-ninth* Day of *September* and *twenty-fifth* ——Day of *March* ———— the firft

Payment thereof to begin and be made on the *twenty-ninth* Day of *September* next enfuing the Day of the Date of thefe Prefents. Witnefs their Hands the

Day and Year firft above-written.

~~Singed in the Prefence of~~

Signed by the said John Sparrow in the presence of

James Brindley

Hugh Henshall

Signed by the said Wm William Cross in the presence of

The signatures of James Brindley, Hugh Henshall and John Sparrow

Harecastle Tunnels. Brindley's right, Telford's on the left.

The construction of the Staffordshire and Worcestershire Canal proceeded at the same time as the Trent and Mersey Canal, as they were to join at Great Haywood, to the east of Stafford. At this point the River Sow, which has taken in the River Penk, enters the River Trent, while the Staffordshire and Worcestershire Canal follows the line of the Rivers Sow, Penk and Stour to the River Severn. The navigation was opened a few months before Brindley's death and its branch to Birmingham was completed just six days before that untimely event. Fortunately, the early records of the Staffordshire and Worcestershire Canal, including the Levelling Books and Day Books, are now on film, providing a brief insight into the methods employed on a pioneering scheme for which there were no reference books and whose whole operation was learned as the work progressed. Unfortunately, the records do not include details, diagrams or continuity for a sample reconstruction of cut, lock or bridge.

Firstly, the landowners and the measurements of the land affected by the cutting of the canal were recorded in the 'Landowners' Dimension Book', and among the many owners of parcels of land were Viscount Dudley, the Earl of Stamford, from Enville, Earl Gower, from Trentham, and a John Hodgetts, Esq., who will be mentioned again in connection with John Brindley. The record of measurements shows that the person employed, probably John Fennyhouse Green, the Under Clerk of the Works, had some knowledge of surveying or geometry, for he used the term *'trapezium base'* and entered the figures in neat columns.

A view of Stourport in 1802

Worsley Old Hall - the scene of many of the meetings between the Duke, Brindley and Gilbert

Worsley New Hall built by Francis Egerton, 3rd Duke of Bridgewater

Trentham, the home of Earl Gower

It was decided at a General Meeting at the Red Lyon in Wolverhampton that a book of Mr Brindley's orders should be kept and signed by him, but the signatures are not uniform. Brindley signed sometimes, but Mr Baker, the Clerk of the Works, may have signed on Brindley's behalf. Mr John Baker kept the book from 17 March 1767, '*...for Inspection at all times by every inferior officer whom it may concern*'. A record of '*Orders given by Mr Brindley to me*' follows, and by 19 March 1767, Mr Brindley was ordering measurements to be taken and a number of instructions continue '*By Mr Baker's orders*' as he supervised the execution of Brindley's requirements. However, there is a possibility that the occasional signature was that of Brindley's nephew of the same name. He trained with his uncle (see chapter 7).

At this time, the drains at Compton, near Wolverhampton, were being set out and a lock sunk at Wightwick Mill, where Mr Thomas Dadford was to have the timber ready, as the locks at Wightwick Mill were sunk under his direction: '*30 April 1767, Order signed by James Brindley*'. Thomas Dadford of Wolverhampton was a carpenter before his canal work as were many of the skilled men on the construction. They were accustomed to measuring, calculating and solving practical problems. However, some work was not up to the required standard and the towing wall through Wightwick Bridge had to be taken down and rebuilt '*by a proper Hand*'. By the end of March 1767 locks at Dimmingsdale, near Wolverhampton, were '*already cut half the depth* [but were] *not to be cut deeper before materials for 'em are ready*'.

Financial estimates were an important consideration and the records refer to such details as the cost of a '*Rock cutting ...2 feet from the Bottom where deep to be 3d per Yard Extra*', and '*Measure 6th April following Rock in field beyond to be all at 3d per Yard Extra; above Soil Price*'. Here the site was close to land owned by Earl Gower.

James Brindley was well aware of the importance of his relationship with the landowners of the estates he bisected. Often the owners were men of influence and some could be difficult. If fences were removed, they were replaced by new ones. In 1768 houses were taken down at Whittington and the '*spoil*', or rubble, spread over boggy land, making good use of all waste. It can be sensed that every effort was made to be tidy and careful about the work and its effect upon the river running parallel to the undertaking. On 13 April 1767 the following was entered in the book: '*Ordered by Mr Brindley to take Notice of the Soil cast out of the Canal near Mr Tong's Piece is likely to fall into the River below then to take Dimensions of the breadth of the River there and set it out so much wider on the other side if necessary ...Was unnecessary*'. Sometimes the water of the River Stour had to be redirected, as opposite Mr Wilmott's orchard. The bottom of the new course was found to be a foot too high with mud and sand, but this was expected to be washed away when the river was turned through it.

Mr John Hodgetts allowed them to dig as deeply as was thought necessary on his land near The Stewponey, close to Kinver. Care had been taken in the felling of trees by the '*Esquire's own men*' so that the site was cleared of undergrowth and trees before the digging began on 15 May 1767. On the same day William Wright, who was later employed on the Birmingham Canal Navigation, signed the following note: '*...before Mr Brindley ...I do hereby promise to make the Bank Water Tight I have now under hand near the Sheep Walk and up to Mr Powell's of Green Forge*.' Brindley also instructed that it was *'Mr Dadford's sole employ to attend to the building of the Lockes'*, and that the sawing was to be done by a qualified carpenter. James Brindley met Mr Baker on 18 July 1767 and gave measurements and instructions at the culvert at Hinkesford, where a well was to be deepened and a water course cut. The record of 5 March 1768: *'Drove a Bottom Stake for a Drain for Shepherd's Cutting in Mr Knight's Meadow next above Austcliff'*, is followed by an entry which shows that long days were worked, even when the hours of winter daylight were few: *'Same Evening had Mr Brindley into Reynold's Cutting against the Sheep Walk who directed me to measure the whole cutting from the Drain to the top at a single depth, to measure the cutting likewise of the new Water courses and allow him wheeling for Do. [ditto] Also to allow him ¹/₄ [d] per yard for Banking on Acct [account] of it's being so well made and 3¹/₂ d per yard for the great rooty Hedge he got out opposite Mr Colbourne's lowermost Meadow'*. More orders were received from Mr Brindley two days later.

On 10 March 1768, Mr Brindley ordered, *'...that the Banks at Giggety to be made 2 yards more than the present width at each end with coarse Gravel or Stones as likewise at every other place in the said Banks where is any appearance of Leaking as likewise the Banks there to be raised 5 or 6 Inches ...with paving or other large stones a coat of marl or clay of same thickness over it and the whole covered with good Gravel'*. Five days later, on 15 March 1768, Mr Thomas Dadford, the carpenter and joiner already employed on the locks, was given a contract for five years *'to serve us in the way of his Trade'*.

In 1767, Mr Baker was *'...to inform himself of what Bridges & where to be built will be most necessary'*, and later the Levelling Book kept by John Fennyhouse Green reads: *'Saw Mr Baker this morning in Shepherd's Work who told me to set Harry on with some men to wheel the spoil to the side of the Canal and of the field where was designed to have been an Arch Bridge a little above Kidderminster and when the above Spoil if got off, the Fence to be made good again and ordered me to set out a Bason for Boats to turn in In field, adjoining to the swivel Bridge in Esq Foley's Brickiln piece below Broadwater & etc'*. The latter swivel bridge may have been the now extinct swing bridge referred to as Bridge No 18 (Langford, 1974). Swing bridges, which were unusual, opened for boats, whereas turnabout or roving bridges were devised to enable the towing horse to cross over without being unhitched when the towpath changed sides.

In 1768 references were made to *'benches'* or bench marks, which mark the elevation on a post or stone, such as those by an old hog sty and a young topped elm by Mr Map's drain. Another was by a stubble field and on a hawthorn tree, *'...in a hedge level with a top water stake near there put in by Mr Simcock'*, the carpenter who had been married to Brindley's sister, Esther, for nearly twenty years. It was found that Mr Map had not cut accurately, so that he had to correct the towing side and *'pun'*, or pound, rubble for three yards behind. Another part of the construction was half a yard too narrow.

During January 1769, *'The Lock chamber at the Hide [The Hyde Kinver] is being finished, and the Gates hung to be full seventy four feet in the clear within.'* There was also a reference to the boats: *'Found length of a Boat lying at upperend of the Tunnelling at Dunsley from the extream [sic] part of her stern atop sixty nine feet five Inches Length of her Rudder 3ft 8in. Total Length 73ft 1in. Found length of another vessell lying in the Stewponey*

Lock from extream parts of her Head and Stern Atop 69 feet Length of her Rudder 3ft 9in. Total Length 72ft 9in. Length of above Lock Chamber in the Clear full, seventy four Feet. Signed by James Brindley'. This must have been a check, for the length of the narrow boats would have been determined from the beginning and before Thomas Dadford began constructing the locks in 1767.

During 1769 work progressed in the area around Mill Street in Kidderminster. On 9 January 1769 Mr JF Green reported in his book of *'Orders from Mr Brindley'*, that there was a great deal of activity with moles, which were disturbing the earth near Kidderminster, because orders to employ a mole catcher had not been followed. At the same time, there were too many soft and useless bricks being used and the person responsible for checking them was threatened with dismissal, as the poorest bricks should have been wheeled to the lock. On the following day, one of the few references to clay was noted, for holes at the bottom of the canal at Austcliff Rock were to be *'well rammed with Clay'*.

In May 1769 brief reference was made to bridge construction; the breadth of the bridge, the height and thickness of the parapet walls, the foundations, buttresses, piles and brickwork requiring, *'Ten thousands of Bricks'*. The height of the arch should allow a man to ride under it. Mr Green must have been familiar with bridge construction although he misspelled the term 'voussoir', meaning the wedge-shaped stones of the arch.

The next order was for *'...a plan and Elevation with proper sections of the above Bridge for Mr Brindley's Inspection against his next coming'*. This is a further record that Brindley worked with plans drawn by others. The tone of the order sounded as though he expected to see them. By the following month the valuable Mr Dadford was to, *'...instruct Mr Pyott in the setting out of bridges as Mr Dadford's sole employ shall be to attend to the building of the locks'*. Brindley saw to it that his men received good training, so that he did not need to be in attendance the whole time.

In the same year work proceeded at the confluence of the Rivers Severn and Stour, where a new town, Stourport, grew out of two villages called Upper and Lower Mitton. Here Brindley devised basins followed by locks so that the canal water was not affected by the variability of the depth of the water of the River Severn, which is soon increased by rainfall in the mountains of Wales, even to flood level. There was tunnelling at Upper Mitton, and Mr Green, *'...afterward went down to Stour's Mouth to engage a Boat as I intend sounding the Ford there as well as the next below tomorrow'*. Mr Green amended Brindley's readings for he thought, *'...a small difference might happen in taking the depth of the soundings to an Exactness ...for the lower sill of the Lock into Severn to lie below the highest part of the 2 channels below I wou'd allow 5 yards'*.

At this time Mr Green sent a letter to James Brindley through Kidderminster Post Office, and it can be seen how he and Mr Dadford were able to communicate with Brindley, even when the engineer was away on other business. The instruction and letter were as follows:

'A drain Trunk to be fixed under the Banking to be made in the Holloway between Evans's and Broad's Gardens at Upper Mitton and no burr or any other matter laid in on the upper side'.

Sir,

Above is Copy of an order you made on 8th Instant in respect to the above places, no mention being made whether a valve or a Plug shou'd be fixed in the Trunk, Mr Dadford and I both thought sometime since that a Plug wou'd be best, as the surface of the Holloway lies 15 feet below top Water there.

We yesterday met Mr Baker in the Work near the Stewponey (having by his Orders been up to Compton to set out the summitt Lock there) who directed me to write to you, and to have you consider whether the method he proposed of having the upper space in the Holloway filled with Burrs [rough stone] is not best; Mr Dadford proposes (if you think it best) to have a square Plug in the Trunk 9 Inches of a side to be set upright Top of its start to come up to near the surface of the Water and so far into the slope of the Bank as to be out of a Boats way, to be properly secured by framing and furnished with a Barrel and chain for drawing it when necessary, and wou'd carry the top of it no higher than within 3 or 4 Inches of the top water, that it shou'd be out of the way of the hawling Lines. As we must very soon set about making of the Bank there shall wait for your Answer and beg you'll favour me with one, by which means shall be sure of having it the day after its coming there.

I am Sir Your most Obedt. Hble Servt.
JFG [John Fennyhouse Green]
Broad Waters 26 Jan 1769

For Mr Brindley Engineer
To the Care of the Doorkeeper
Of the Honble House of Commons

Obviously, the Clerk and the Under Clerk employed on the construction were able and of a good education, but Brindley was still in charge. He had to 'think it best' before they continued, although he was open to useful suggestions from Mr Baker and the carpenter, Mr Dadford. Brindley must have been at the House of Commons on business for another canal project and his reply indicates that he was in London for some time. Writing on 3 February 1769, Brindley was using the address of Thomas Gilbert, MP, Queen Street, Westminster, and Mr Green was able to copy the following into the record book:

London 3d Febry 1769
Sir
I reced [received] your Favour of the 26th and would have you proceed as directed in the Orders that is, not to lay any Burrs [etc.] as that (if found necessary) may be done afterwards, I wou'd have you make a Plug as you propose, as I apprehend it may be full as well as a valve, as it is so much below the Level - If you want any farther Orders - please to direct for me at Thos. Gilbert's Esq. in Queen Street, Westminster.

P.S. If Mr Baker hath anything   *Sr*
To write please to desire him to   *Your Hble Servt*
direct to me here.   *Jas Brindley*

Mr JF Green immediately made a copy of the relevant part and sent it to Mr Dadford's house. The letter shows that although James Brindley was constantly busy with several projects elsewhere in the country, he was still confident in turning down Mr Baker's suggestion for the time being and accepting that of Mr Dadford without making an urgent visit.

This was the only time that this researcher has noted Brindley using the abbreviation 'Jas.' for James in his signature and, in the light of recent information from the USA, this signature may be that of James Brindley's nephew of the same name, the eldest son of Joseph Brindley of Alton (see Chapter 7).

Public relations were a very important side of the work of canal officials, for there were landowners such as Mr Harper to deal with. Mr Green, the Under Clerk of the Works, was sent down to convince Mr Harper that the top water of the proposed canal would not ruin his garden at Cawdwell Hall [Caldwell]. It was believed that Mr Harper had already given his consent, but by January 1769, he would do so only if, '*Mr Brindley wou'd declare there was an absolute necessity for the Canal being taken thro' his Garden wou'd also give him his Reasons for it and if he then shou'd think so too, he wou'd give his consent otherwise he had rather it was taken the other way. We both used Arguments to convince him ...but all to no purpose*'.

Mr Green wrote to Mr Brindley from Kidderminster on 31 January 1769, relating the above episode adding that it '*...plainly appeared to me he [Mr Harper] wanted a sum of money for his consent ...& [I] beg to know how you wou'd have me proceed*'. Mr Watkins was leaving for London and so he was able to deliver the letter, but due to the length of the journey a reply was just too late to be included in Brindley's letter of 3 February. Unfortunately the filmed record ends at this point and Brindley's answer to Mr Harper has not come to light.

The Staffordshire and Worcestershire Canal was important to the metal industries of South Staffordshire, for it skirted Wolverhampton and Stourbridge, as well as joining the Trent and Mersey Canal at Great Haywood, close to Wolseley Bridge, where the important meeting of 1765 had taken place. The construction of the northern section was in progress in the New Year of 1770 and the record reads: '*Afterwards met with Mr Brindley on Calf Heath and went with him along where the Canal is sett [sic] out from the Street road* [Watling Street, A5] *down to Penkrich* [Penkridge]. *The following is the Orders given and signed by him at Penkrich 12th Jany 1770*':

'*That a temporary Drain be made across the Latherfoote Brooke [Latherford] from end of Buckley's work above to lay it dry, that the Clay in Bowker's Cutting may be got out for making Bricks as soon as possible. The Pumps Water Troughs and Waterwheel with its Appendages and at Kidderminster to be sent up to Goody Bridge and properly deposited in Water, till the Banking there is begun that they will be wanted. The boring Rods to be sent at the same time - 10ft well to be sunk, below the surface of Low ground.*'

This is a rare mention of equipment in these early records.

Shepherd, Bowker, Buckley, Map, and others were each in charge of a section of cutting and Brindley, known for his economical methods, wasted nothing from the cast out materials, be they stones, earth or clay. The clay from Bowker's cutting was drained and used for making bricks for the work in hand, but a constant supply of the cold, sticky substance was required for '*the puddling*'.

The quotations selected above were chosen for their references either to Brindley or an interesting aspect of the project, for none give a complete picture of the procedures of the construction. Brindley was thought to have experimented with locks at a model canal in the grounds of his home, the locks on the Staffordshire and Worcestershire Canal being his first, but the records make no reference to the idea. Apart from *'puddle the Ramparting'* in August 1767, there were few references to puddling or the number of labourers employed, except for an order for Reynolds not to engage more than twenty men in making banks at a culvert on 17th April 1767. Meteyard mentioned the employment of 600 men at a time on building the first ten miles of the Trent and Mersey Canal. (Records of the Staffordshire and Worcestershire Canal contractors have not been examined here.)

The Committee declared that the 46 miles of the Staffordshire and Worcestershire Canal were open for trade on 28 May 1772, but the record book shows that Brindley's work had finished before that date, *'...that Mr James Brindley be discharged at Michmas* [Michaelmas] *next* (before 17 March 1772)'. The record books began on 17 March 1767, five years from the limit in 1772, but the next Michaelmas Day was 29 September 1771 when presumably all the major construction work requiring Brindley's attention was complete. He visited the sites fairly regularly at the beginning. There seems to have been a monthly attendance, especially during 1767, and occasionally a day or two together, but as the plans were set out and the building progressed without serious problems, his visits became less frequent. However, the above letters show that he could communicate with those in charge at the site and they did not proceed without his permission even in the fourth year of the project. Brindley was attending to the problems at Harecastle at the same time as the Staffordshire and Worcestershire Canal and other developments, such as the Birmingham Canal Navigation, the Droitwich, the Coventry and the Oxford Canals. Some thought that he was not giving them enough attention and after a disagreement his employment as Surveyor of the Coventry Canal was terminated.

Brindley was required to survey canals in several parts of the country and according to Wedgwood he was planning a visit to Scotland and Ireland. Wedgwood had been concerned about the engineer's health since 2 March 1767, shortly before the Staffordshire and Worcestershire Canal's Order Book began. Wedgwood was of the opinion that James Brindley was, *'...so incessantly harassed on every side, that he hath no rest, either for his mind, or Body, & will not be prevailed upon to take proper care of his health'*. Wedgwood wrote that Brindley had become an object of pity, *'...a real sufferer for the good of the Public'*, and *'...may get a few thousand'*, but then, surprisingly, described his old friend as *'money getting'*. By 2 April 1767, James Brindley was not well enough to attend a meeting of the Committee and General Assembly of the Grand Trunk project.

It was September before the Brindleys managed to go to Buxton and Matlock for a break, but Wedgwood wrote that Mr & Mrs Brindley had little rest as he was *'...known everywhere & cannot retire'*. The holiday improved the situation, but Wedgwood thought that James Brindley required more than a fortnight's rest, little realising that he was actually developing his final illness. Brindley's interests on holiday were such that he made observations on lead mining methods near Matlock, noting particularly what the miners did with the residue from the operation. Friends of Wedgwood were always on the lookout for geological specimens and fossils as he was keen to experiment with new materials for his pottery clay as well as following the popular interest in geology.

It was September 1768 before Brindley was able to make the long journey to Scotland to give an opinion on Smeaton's plans for the Forth and Clyde Canal and also on Golborne's survey of the harbour at Glasgow. The printed Extracts from the Records of the Burgh of Glasgow record the payment of £5 18s sterling to, *'Baillie John Gray as the expense debursed by him as a survey of the harbour at Port Glasgow and the river Clyde, by Messrs, Brindley and Goburne* [Golborne], *engineers employed by the toun* [town] *to make the said survey, conform to a particular account bearing date September 1768'.* Payments were made to another engineer for installing a *'horse engine'* and pumps for the dry dock. John Smeaton's review of the navigation and *'Observations on the reports of Messrs, Brindley, Yeomans and Golborn'*, (1768) are preserved in the British Library, London. During the visit, Smeaton made his 'hobby horse' remark in reference to Brindley's aqueducts, but the building of the Forth and Clyde Canal was to have a history of delays and Smeaton died before its completion. The task was finished by Brindley's pupil, Robert Whitworth.

James Brindley's descendants possess a Burgess Ticket granted to him by the Council of the City of Glasgow on 9 September 1768, meaning that he was received as a Burgess or Guild Brother. As an Honorary Burgess he did not have to pay admission dues or receive privileges such as a say in Council matters. A Roll of Burgesses was kept before 1730, but so many were being given that records ceased. The recipients must have rendered a service to the town and the more distinguished of them, such as James Brindley, were given an ornate document. The artist or painter received £10-8s on 26 September 1768 and may have produced several for that sum. A quotation from the Burgesses and Guild Brethren of Glasgow (1925) mentions that the Council enjoyed the occasions, *'...as affording agreeable opportunities for conviviality, speech making and drinking healths'.*

Apart from work on the Duke of Bridgewater's canal, the first of Brindley's canals, the six mile long Droitwich Canal, was opened for trade on 12 March 1771. On 7 May 1769, a letter from Droitwich asked for one hundred and fifty plans to be sent to the Navigation Office in Birmingham but although supposedly written and signed by James Brindley, the handwriting, numbers and signature do not match those in his notebook or the marriage register. Similarities with his wife's writing and a flourish on her will suggest that the letter was her work and the phrase *'please to direct'* occurs in the February letter from London, too. It was in the style of the time and tradition has it that Ann wrote letters for her husband occasionally. Again, it is possible that Brindley's nephew of the same name wrote letters and signed messages for his uncle, who usually wrote his name in full and not in the abbreviated form 'Jas. Brindley'. Thomas Allen, another nephew of Uncle James, was also employed in the canal business.

Brindley's brother-in-law Samuel Simcock, once a carpenter in Leek, became a trusted assistant engineer and worked on the Staffordshire and Worcestershire Canal, the Birmingham Canal and the Oxford Canal. From time to time, committee members of the latter gave James Brindley some difficulty, but he backed his brother-in-law when the winding route invited criticism. In 1772, Samuel Simcock took over as engineer of the Oxford Canal after Brindley's death and remarks suggested that he was imprinting his initials on the countryside. He had followed Brindley's method of avoiding expensive cuttings and structures, and the animosity of landowners. The route was intended to serve as many places and businesses as possible. However, several sections were straightened in the 18th century. This researcher lived by one such section for a time and a raised and fertile part of the garden contained the thick blue clay from the old puddling. Simcock was involved with the Kennet and Avon Canal, which opened in 1810. A small canal museum, in a house near Aldermaston, displays a list of surveys dated 17 July 1794. It mentions Simcock with Barnes and Weston in 1789. In the same year, Robert Whitworth, also trained by Brindley, queried the water supply. In the following year, *'John Rennie sees no water supply problem. 3rd March 1790 go ahead.'*

T Baddeley's research found that Brindley had a family connection with yet another of his trainees. Josiah Clowes was a carpenter who inherited Catherine Fields, in Norton-in-the-Moors, from his bachelor uncle Josiah. The latter was a landowner and coalmaster at Whitfield, close to the site of the water engine mentioned here earlier. Josiah junior's older brother, William Clowes, married Jane Henshall at Wolstanton in 1749/50 and Hugh Henshall witnessed Josiah's wedding at Norton-in-the-Moors in 1762. Josiah's young bride died six weeks later and was buried in Norton churchyard. It was 1765 before Brindley married young Ann Henshall, sister to Jane and Hugh.

Josiah Clowes became a respected canal engineer, beginning his career on the Harecastle Tunnel project. Charles Hadfield's study mentioned that Josiah Clowes was a carrier on the Trent and Mersey Canal, but was dismissed *'for inattention to duty,'* when working on the Chester Canal construction in 1775. Apparently he had other work, but the Chester Committee thought that he should give their project his full attention. Josiah Clowes died in 1795. He had worked alongside Robert Whitworth, surveyed for the Birmingham and Worcester Canal and been the engineer for the Dudley Canal and the Shrewsbury Canal. His tunnelling experience took him to the Sapperton Tunnel. In 1795, Thomas Telford took the place of Josiah Clowes as engineer in Shropshire. It is interesting to note that following a flood, Telford replaced some of the traditional masonry of Clowes with iron from the powerful Shropshire ironmasters, who were closely involved with the canals in that county.

Material in the British Library includes Brindley's 1771 survey of the River Thames between Monkey Island and Isleworth, and from Boulter's Lock to Mortlake, with a *'section'* of the river. There are also Brindley's answers to queries of the Committee of the Common Council of the City of London in 1770, as landowners raised objections. Other queries concern his report on the drainage of the Fens, near Wisbech.

As mentioned previously, Wedgwood expressed the need for a new plate for printing a revised plan. Brindley recommended Mr Oldham of Manchester as, *'...a proper Person to lay it down anew'*. Some years later, on 27 April 1769, a plan was published by and for James Brindley, and it bears the heading: *'Plan of the Navigable Canals now making in the Inland Parts of this Kingdom, for opening a Communication to the*

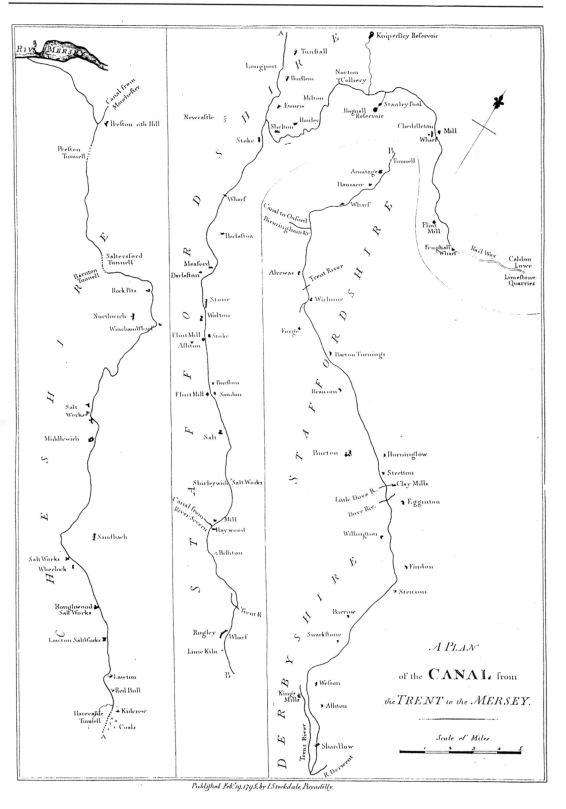

Plan of the Trent and Mersey Canal (1795)

Ports of London, Bristol, Liverpool and Hull with the adjacent TOWNS and RIVERS, by JAMES BRINDLEY, Engineer', and below it reads: *'To the most Noble Francis, Duke of BRIDGEWATER Marquis of Brackley & Baron Ellesmere. This PLAN is most Humbly Dedicated By his Grace's most Obedt. humble Servt. James Brindley'*. Such a dedication confirmed Brindley's position and acknowledged the respect he had for the Duke, a man Wedgwood found, *'...had the same affable, familiar manner as usual, when he first began to know us, by ourselves in Propia Persona, & not from his go betweens'*.

Brindley was by no means the first to think of inland navigation, but the success of the Triumvirate, followed by the determined promotion by Brindley and Wedgwood of the 'Grand Cross' plan to link four ports, led to the Canal Age. Wedgwood sometimes wrote six letters a day about navigation in addition to his normal work. He was responsible for the promotional pamphlets written by his friend Bentley, but edited by Dr Darwin. Brindley's increasing knowledge of commerce from the Duke and *'the Staffordshire men'* made him well aware of the requirements of the plan, which Wedgwood saw as *'...the Uniteing of Seas and distant countrys'*. Even in 1766, the potter explained that the bulk of his ware was exported to Europe, North America and the West Indies. It is interesting that Wedgwood's letter of 18 July 1766 mentioned that he had *'a map of rivers'*, whereas Brindley's knowledge came from the fact that his home was near the watershed of two great river systems. Brindley probably saw Wedgwood's map several times, but the practical geography lesson was on his own doorstep, as the River Trent and its tributaries flow southward from the moorlands, while the River Dane meanders westward to the system of the Rivers Weaver and Mersey. Following a river was an obvious method of finding a direction and Brindley would have seen the Severn at Coalbrookdale, the navigable Trent at Nottingham, the value of the Mersey at Liverpool in his work for the Duke of Bridgewater and the Thames on his visits to London.

As a natural geographer James Brindley surveyed hundreds of miles of countryside in areas previously unknown to him, but the observations and abilities developed in his native hills and dales were the foundation of such work. According to Rees, Brindley journeyed to Scotland, County Durham, Yorkshire, Preston, Lancaster, Liverpool, Chester, Somerset, Devon, Wiltshire, Hampshire and London. The route of the Chesterfield Canal was his final survey, apart from the preliminary ride for the Caldon Canal branch on which he was taken ill at Froghall, near Ipstones. Canal history is complex, for there were so many interested parties; the committees, businessmen, landowners, rival routes, the problems of finance, and the employment of engineers, contractors and their men, who became known as 'navigators' or 'navvies', the carpenters and boatbuilders. With only a very small number keeping records, the system was learned as the undertakings progressed. It was to the credit of all concerned that the work proceeded at such a rate. As every canal presented individual features, it was Brindley's role as consultant engineer and his exceptional confidence in projecting canals that became so important. Such confidence inevitably invited some criticism, but it was essential for the development of large scale plans.

Wedgwood's letters and obituary show that James Brindley had the qualities of a professional, with honesty, dedication, the ability to leave instructions and facilities

The canal warehouses of Gilbert, Henshall & Co

TOWN-HALL & MARKET-HOUSE OF BURSLEM.

Burslem, early 18th century. It was an important and busy centre of new trade.

for the training of others. He solved problems by his own observation and the minimum of equipment, but Bentley's reference to his remarkable memory recalled how he used to plan and calculate in the quietness of his bed, even for days at a time. Modern students know the value of study in the isolation of the bedroom, and yet in Brindley's time, it was considered strange that he required such concentrated effort. Years after Brindley's death, A. Kippis received letters containing anecdotes of the engineer for an encyclopaedia, but he was uncertain of their authenticity and they have not been repeated here. Wedgwood's letter recorded an occasional saying of Brindley, such as on 5 March 1768, when he remarked, *'I am every day more fully convinced of the justness of our frd* [friend] *Brindley's Maxim that where application is expected, - 'Half bred things are the best'.*

There were signs of Brindley having an awkward temper at times, for he quarrelled with Gilbert when both wished to pursue their respective parts of the construction to the inconvenience of the other and then again when Brindley believed his mare was in foal by Gilbert's horse, as it seriously interfered with his means of transport. Brindley's message was, *'No more society'*, but the situation was temporary. The Birmingham Navigation Committee complained that he did not visit them enough when obviously he had taken on too much work. His disagreements with the Committees of the Oxford and Coventry Canals led to the termination of his employment with the latter construction. Negotiations with so many Committees and interested parties were bound to be fraught with difficulties at times. Brindley did not always see eye to eye with the engineer, John Smeaton, although they came together to give opinions on a number of schemes. When the canal was being set out in front of Etruria Hall in December 1767, Wedgwood and Henshall made sure that they adhered to Brindley's instruction or, *'Mr Brindley would go mad'*. How much of this temperament was inherited from his father and grandfather, who had to be curbed for some reason, even by wills, how much was stress from the responsibility and how much was due to a developing and incurable illness can only be guessed. Wedgwood described him as a *'sensible friend and an affectionate husband'*.

Eventually, the Institution of Civil Engineers was formed in London and in 1828 a charter was drawn up in which civil engineering was described as the *'art of directing the sources of power in nature for the use and convenience of man... as applied in the construction of roads, aqueducts, canals, river navigation and docks ...ports, harbours, ...and etc'*. Mechanical engineering was concerned with steam engines, mill work and moving machinery. James Brindley was associated with several of these branches when the term 'engineer' was just beginning to be used. Large scale projects under his direction were to have far reaching consequences and his mechanical inventions eased problems as they arose, so that John Ward of Stoke-on-Trent went as far as naming Brindley *'The Father of Engineers'*. Perhaps the true evaluation of Brindley's work should be left to engineers, for the memoranda of Committees only provide a partial record. The narrow tunnel at Harecastle began to show inconveniences. Original work often combines success and some misjudgements to be improved upon. Brindley's greatest achievement was the foundation of the inland waterways system, linking the ports in a *'Grand Cross'*.

CHAPTER 4
PRIVATE LIFE

James Brindley seemed to have little time for domestic life and it must have been a surprise to his family and friends when, at the age of forty-nine, he married the teenage daughter of John Henshall, a surveyor and colleague from Newchapel, in the parish of Wolstanton. It was still a period when marriages were often 'arranged', but the couple appeared to be happy. When business took him to her father's house, Brindley offered gingerbread as a treat for Ann when she was still a schoolgirl. Her father was well-known in the district. In 1752, John Henshall added his neat signature to the will of Mrs Jemima Stevenson, an aunt of Burslem Wedgwood. In 1756, Thomas Wedgwood and John Henshall were executors of the lengthy will of Catherine Egerton, a great-aunt of Josiah Wedgwood. Henshall's wife was left five pounds and a squab, or large cushion, from a parlour at the Wedgwood property of the Overhouse.

The marriage bond for Brindley's wedding carried John Henshall's consent for his daughter's marriage and although the document implies that the bridegroom appeared personally when the application for a licence was made, the signature of James Brindley does not bear his usual 'J' or 'e'. The bachelor 'engineer of Leek' was of age and Ann was said to be twenty years old. However, she was younger, unless her baptism at Newchapel on 23 April 1747 had been delayed. On 8 December 1765, at St Margaret's Church, Wolstanton, the bride and groom signed the register in good handwriting; Brindley used his old style 'e' and Ann added an 'e' to her name, although it was not so at her baptism.

The couple lived near to the Henshalls and Wedgwood and his wife visited them at Newchapel. Turnhurst in Newchapel was the mansion long accepted as Brindley's home during his marriage, although proof of his tenancy has not been found. Ownership, lease, tenancy and undertenancy are complex areas to research. The deed of 1772, mentioned here previously, refers to a piece of Turnhurst land which was lately in the holding or occupation of Thomas Tunstall, his undertenants or assigns. Brindley had been a shareholder in the Newchapel/Goldenhill district since 1760. Turnhurst was a mere one and a half miles from Harecastle and was described by Smiles as a *'comfortable, roomy, old fashioned dwelling, with a garden and a pleasure garden behind, and a little lake in front'*. There were distant views from the many windows. A daughter was born to the middle-aged engineer and his young wife on 17 December 1769. She was baptised on 3 January 1770 and named Ann(e) after her Henshall grandmother. The ceremony probably took place at home as the Newchapel register records that the child was 'admitted' on 4 August 1770. This suggests that the baby was not strong at birth. On 6 January 1772 a daughter, Susanna(h), was born and named after her Brindley grandmother, but this baby was not baptised until 27 December 1772, three months after the death of her father.

James Brindley must have spent limited time with his family as he was extremely busy and far from well. Josiah Wedgwood had been concerned about the

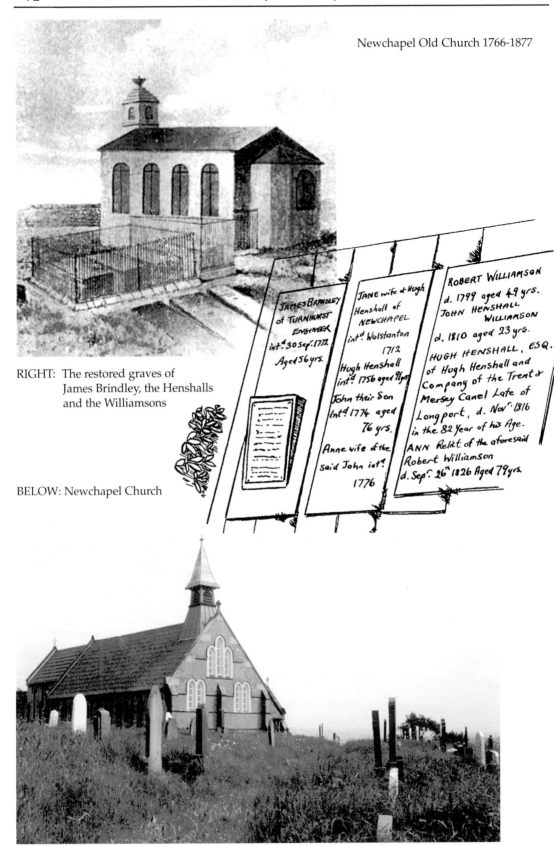

Newchapel Old Church 1766-1877

RIGHT: The restored graves of
James Brindley, the Henshalls
and the Williamsons

BELOW: Newchapel Church

JAMES BRINDLEY
of TURNHURST
ENGINEER
int.d 30 Sep: 1772
Aged 56 yrs.

JANE wife of Hugh
Henshall of
NEWCHAPEL
int.d Wolstanton
1712
Hugh Henshall
int.d 1756 aged 9lyrs
John their Son
int.d 1774 aged
76 yrs.
Anne wife of the
said John int.d
1776

ROBERT WILLIAMSON
d. 1799 aged 49 yrs.
JOHN HENSHALL
WILLIAMSON
d. 1810 aged 23 yrs.
HUGH HENSHALL, ESQ.
of Hugh Henshall and
Company of the Trent &
Mersey Canel Late of
Longport, d. Nov.r 1816
in the 82 Year of his Age.
ANN Relict of the aforesaid
Robert Williamson
d. Sep.r 26.th 1826 Aged 79 yrs.

Turnhurst, Brindley's home 1765-1772

engineer's health for some years and had urged him to rest. During the summer of 1772, the trouble was diagnosed as diabetes by the eminent Dr Erasmus Darwin of Lichfield. The doctor would have been unable to give any effective treatment with the herbs and concoctions available at that time and Brindley's condition was aggravated by his lifestyle of overwork and irregular meals. He finally succumbed when provided with damp bedding at an inn at Ipstones, less than four miles from the home of his aged mother at Lowe Hill and that of his brother, Joseph, at Alton. James Brindley had been riding through the woods of the pretty Churnet valley, making an initial survey for the Caldon Canal to Froghall and the limestone supplies of Cauldon. He stayed at the inn, probably with a tired horse, but Brindley himself was more than tired; he was very ill.

Wedgwood realised that there was little hope for the patient and wrote to his friend Thomas Bentley that he had visited Brindley at Turnhurst nearly every day that week, but can give '*...but a melancholy account ...Poor Mr Brindley has nearly finish'd his course in this world. He says he must leave us, & indeed I do not expect to find him alive in the morning'*. The letter revealed that James Brindley had suffered the fever and thirst of diabetes for seven years. The symptoms may have begun earlier, for it will be recalled that he returned to his bed at an inn when the filling of the Barton Aqueduct caused him anxiety and he had taken time to recover from seeing a play in London; both situations when emotion affected him physically. Now it is known that the blood sugar level of diabetics can be adversely affected by stress.

Wedgwood said that Mrs Brindley was inconsolable and had difficulty taking rest or food. He had a word with her and she '*...has promis'd me to exert herself in bearing his afflicting stroke all in her power for the sake of her Aged Parents & her helpless Children'*. Ann was then twenty-five and her daughters were only babes under two-and-a-half years old.

Wedgwood told his friend that the illness, '*...will deprive us of a valuable friend, & the world of one of those great Genius's who seldom live to see justice done to their singular* *abilities, but must trust to future ages for that tribute of praise & fair fame they so greatly merit from their fellow mortals'.* Tradition has it that the canal builders had even come to his death bed for advice, but all he could tell them was to, *'Puddle it again and again.'* Wedgwood's next letter recorded that James Brindley had died on 27 September 1772, *'...about 12 at noon, in a sound sleep, for about 3 o'clock in the morning, after giving him somthing to wet his mouth, he said, 'its enough - I shall need no more', shut his Eyes, never more to open, he continued to the time of his death, (about 9 hours) seemingly in a fine sleep, & yielded up his breath at last without a single groan'.*

The letter continued with Wedgwood's appraisal of a man for whom he had great respect and had known for many years, describing him as a sensible friend and an affectionate husband, but with a mind *'...too ardently intent upon the execution of the works it had plann'd ... for which Millions yet unborn will revere & bless his memory.'* He suggested that Bentley should send a report to some of the papers and thought that the Duke of Bridgewater *'...might & indeed ought to have a handsome compliment paid to him on this occasion, to encourage others to bring Genius to light & support its first efforts, as he has nobly done'.* Wedgwood knew Gilbert well, but he did not mention him.

Josiah Wedgwood informed Dr Erasmus Darwin of the death of his patient and the doctor replied that he would have attended immediately if he had known Brindley's condition had worsened. It was he who encouraged Hugh Henshall to write something of the engineer's life.

The *Gentleman's Magazine* (vol. 92) announced Brindley's death briefly, *'the celebrated engineer, who projected the Duke of Bridgewater's navigation.'* On 5 October 1772, *Aris's Gazette* of Birmingham included a long obituary, probably written by Bentley, for whole sentences are reminiscent of Wedgwood's letter: *'What the Public has lost can only be conceived by those who best knew his Character and Talents. To those Talents and his truly noble patron the Duke of Bridgewater this Age and Nation are indebted for the works ...Mr Brindley had long been sensible of the precarious Situation of his Health and wishing to be succeeded in his Profession by his brother-in-law, Mr Henshall, Clerk of the Works of the Grand Trunk Navigation, he spared no Pains to qualify him for that important Trust...'*

Hugh Henshall supported his sister in her bereavement. Most likely Brindley was taken quietly to the hilltop graveyard within sight of his home, by his widow, the Henshalls, John Brindley and, almost certainly, Josiah Wedgwood. Whether canal officials, business clients, brothers, sisters and his aged mother were able to attend is not known. Brindley's 'table tomb' in Newchapel Churchyard was surrounded by metal railings, as were those of his widow's family in the same row. After nearly two hundred years, restoration was required and the stones were laid flat at ground level without railings. Brindley's gravestone lies alongside that of Ann's Henshall grandparents and his widow is recorded on the next but one stone, with her second husband, their drowned son and her brother.

In 1956, the restoration was funded by public subscription and a plaque for Brindley's grave was presented by EJD Warrilow FSA, Staffordshire County Secretary of the Ancient Monument Society. The plaque records the main events in Brindley's life, but inexplicably, gives the date of death as 25 September 1772, although Wedgwood's letter of the 28th stated that death occurred on the *'27th Inst. about 12 at*

Noon'. In the elegant lettering of the period, the gravestone reads:

JAMES BRINDLEY
of TURNHURST
ENGINEER
was interr'd Sepr 30th 1772
Aged 56

Hugh Henshall attended to the legal and financial affairs of Brindley's young family, including the signing of documents in which Ann renounced her right to attend to the administration of Brindley's estate. The engineer had not left a will and Hugh and the solicitors were 'bound' in the sum of £14,000, which was usually double the estimated value of the estate, but there is no inventory or exact record of Brindley's affairs. The engineer's resources had increased rapidly as many demands were made on him and he was being paid for schemes running concurrently. He had not even attended to the estate of his deceased father and probate was not granted on that until the following year, 1773. Pressure of work must have been the reason. By December 1772, Hugh Henshall, as the legal guardian of Brindley's two little daughters, concluded the arrangements for their benefit.

Wedgwood collected material for the memoir, but a few words from the Duke of Bridgewater, John Gilbert and others would have been useful. Dr Darwin composed a long poem, but talk of *'nymphs'* and *'weeping Naiads'* seems unsuited to Brindley and the doctor's suggestion of a statue in Westminster Abbey came to nothing. In fact, it was 218 years before a statue of Brindley was erected anywhere. On Friday, 20 July 1990, a celebration of his life took place by the side of the Caldon Canal at Etruria, close to its junction with the Trent and Mersey Canal and less than a mile from where Wedgwood's factory once stood.

Wedgwood's Works at Etruria

Brindley's statue at Etruria, Stoke-on-Trent,
in the new marina (1990)

The day of the unveiling was unusually hot. The civic dignitaries in formal dress, schoolchildren in 18th-century style costumes and the Schools' Brass Band sweltered as they waited for the arrival of Lord Hesketh and other guests by narrowboat. Lord Hesketh performed the unveiling as Parliamentary under Secretary for the Environment, with a special responsibility for waterways. James Brindley's statue stood on its plinth of light coloured stone under a cloth of scarlet satin, until the rather youthful bronze figure was revealed. With his levelling instrument at his side, he looks towards the Trent and Mersey Canal and Wolstanton Church, a short distance across the valley. The joyful occasion continued with a reading of Wedgwood's letter of appreciation, followed by a display of 18th century games by the children of the James Brindley High School, Biddulph.

Shortly before his death, James Brindley agreed to have his portrait painted, but then refused it when he took offence at the way the artist asked for payment. This incident may provide an example of what has been described as Brindley's 'tetchy' temperament, but the poor man was close to death. On 18 September 1772, Josiah Wedgwood received a note from Ann Brindley, asking if he would have a word with Mr Bentley to retrieve the picture as *'She has set her heart much upon having it'*. It was taken to his widow. The portrait does not show Brindley's legs and the legs of the statue had to be 'created' by the sculptor, Mr Colin Melbourne, the Principal of the Sir Henry Doulton School of Sculpture, at Fenton. The portrait by Francis Parsons was on loan to the National Gallery in recent decades, but has been purchased for its permanent collection. In the style of the period, Brindley was given a fine, fair complexion with flushed cheeks and youthful hands, rather than the rugged, bronzed features he would have had from his outdoor life. He wore a wig as expected of a man

Brindley Place in Birmingham

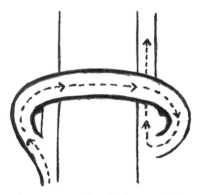

Roving or Turnabout bridges enabled the
towing horses to cross the canal when the
towpath changed sides.

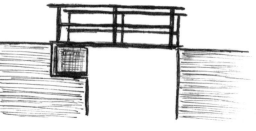

Swing Bridge

Bridges

An old bridge preserved

Old and New in central Birmingham

in his best attire and stood by a large urn of classical style framed with abundant foliage. His right hand was at his hip and his left hand lay relaxed over his levelling instrument. Barton Aqueduct, the River Irwell and sailing ships in the background make a satisfactory combination of indoor formality and outdoor achievement. A portrait by the same artist is in Stoke-on-Trent Art Gallery. Salford Art Gallery has another version, by an unknown artist, in which the features, the hands and the background are different. The Institute of Engineers has a lithograph which has been used in publications for two centuries. Sometimes Brindley is looking to the right and sometimes to the left. Minor changes from the original show in buttons, buttonholes, cuffs and hands, but eyes can never be copied precisely. How did Brindley really look?

From the churchyard where Brindley lies, the southward view overlooks the Turnhurst site. On 10 September 1929, the *Evening Sentinel* expressed regret at the demolition of Turnhurst Hall. Until 1990, only an electricity pylon occupied the rough ground, but new houses and gardens have been built there now. The remains of a water feature in the garden of the old hall was thoroughly excavated by archaeologists, but a popular idea that it was Brindley's model canal, with lock gates, could not be substantiated. It is preserved under a cover of concrete, beneath the car park to a new public house (Klemperer & Sillitoe, 1995). Rectangular fishponds, sometimes called canals, were once fashionable in quite modest gardens and one was labelled as such on a plan of the garden of Brindley's distant family connection, Henry Bradford, at Camp Hill, Birmingham.

JHDM Campbell, a descendant of James Brindley's younger grandson, described the few personal items inherited from his ancestor - a lock of greying hair, a miniature portrait, a seal, the Burgess ticket and an antique Bible given to Brindley by the Duke of Bridgewater (Campbell 1956-59). The Brindley Mill Trust and Museum, in Leek, has a theodolite, or level, and a notebook, while other memoranda books are in London. A photostat copy of the notebook dated 1755-1758 was made from the original loaned to Birmingham Reference Library (now Birmingham Central Library) in 1939.

In 1994, the dedicated work of volunteers responsible for the restoration and development of Brindley's historic mill in Mill Street, Leek was rewarded in the registration of the museum by the Museum and Galleries Commission.

James Brindley School in Birmingham is for children in hospital and for young patients who require home tutoring.

James Brindley is honoured in Birmingham since the redevelopment of a city centre site has been named Brindley Place, beside the Birmingham Canal Navigation. Nearby, a new public house bears his name and a simple memorial of blue bricks stands on the canal-side Brindley Walk. The plaque reads:

THIS CANAL LAID THE FOUNDATION OF
THE BIRMINGHAM CANAL NAVIGATION AND
CONTRIBUTED SIGNIFICANTLY TO THE COMMERCIAL PROSPERITY
OF THE CITY OF BIRMINGHAM 1769-1969

A view towards Stoke, Etruria and Hanley from Basford (1850).

Armitage Park, later Hawkesyard Priory

CHAPTER 5
DAUGHTERS AND DESCENDANTS

The widowed Ann Brindley remained close to her family and her brother, Hugh Henshall, took care of the financial matters. Their aged father, John Henshall, was buried in 1774, having known of the fame and fate of his son-in-law. With two small daughters to bring up Ann married again after three years of widowhood. This time her husband was a little younger than herself.

The bridegroom, Robert Williamson, originally from north Cheshire, described himself on the marriage bond as an engineer of the Parish of Wolstanton, possibly having worked on the Trent and Mersey Canal construction as it neared completion. 'Rob Williamson', who signed his name with an underlining flourish, married Ann on 30 December 1775 at Wolstanton Church. According to a grandson, they lived at Knypersley Hall initially, and three of their children were baptised at Biddulph. One infant died, but by 1780 the family were in Longport, where four more children were born and Robert established a pottery. Ann and Susanna Brindley were brought up with their half-brothers and half-sisters namely, Jane, Mary, Robert and Elizabeth Williamson, Hugh Henshall Williamson, Catherine Williamson and John Henshall Williamson. In 1784, Robert Williamson was listed as a gentleman and a juror to the Tunstall Court, with his brother-in-law, Hugh Henshall, the Wedgwoods and John Rogers, a nephew of John Brindley, all of whom were involved with pottery and canal trade. By 1786, or perhaps earlier, Robert Williamson was a partner in the Goldenhill group; Hugh Henshall would have ensured his inclusion in family business.

James Brindley's younger daughter, Susanna, was married by licence at Burslem Church on 8 December 1795. This day would have been the 30th wedding anniversary of her parents and suggests that she had been brought up to be mindful of her father. On the day preceding the wedding the marriage bond was signed by her stepfather and the bridegroom, Mr John Bettington, a merchant from the Parish of St James, in Bristol. The event was announced in the county newspaper, *The Staffordshire Advertiser,* and the union produced two sons - James Brindley Bettington (b1796) and John Henshall Bettington (b1798) - named after their grandfather and great-grandfather, respectively.

These happy times were soon clouded and illness must have prompted Robert Williamson to make his will on 13 August 1799. On 3 October, he died aged only forty-nine and Brindley's widow was alone again. Robert was buried at Newchapel, close to Ann's parents, grandparents and James Brindley, but the widow's grief was soon doubled, for only two weeks later, Susanna Bettington died aged 27. The tragedy left Brindley's two very young grandsons motherless. Susanna's widower, John Bettington, married again and fathered more children, but he maintained contact with Susanna's family, eventually acting as trustee and executor of Hugh Henshall's lengthy will. He received £50 for his trouble, while his two sons by Susanna were left £50 each as *'Remembrance Legacies'* from their great-uncle Hugh.

John Bettington's business as a merchant extended to London, where his address was J Bettington, Sons & Co, 8 Bank Chambers, Lothbury, in the 1820s and 1830s. By 1840 and 1841, James Brindley's younger grandson, John Henshall Bettington, merchant, was at 13 Great St Helen's, off Bishopsgate. The brothers had followed in their father's footsteps.

In 1827 James Brindley Bettington sailed away to Australia, where his new life began with a plan to establish a trading centre for wool. Captain James Cook had sighted and landed on the eastern coast of the continent two years before the death of Brindley, the engineer. The small settlement of Sydney had become known for its penal colony, where conditions were harsh, rough and dangerous. Some convicts had only committed minor offences through hardship or injustice. Nevertheless, the town of Sydney was beginning to take shape along its coves and inlets, suitable for harbours, sailing ships and wharves, although the development of farming and food production in the vicinity suffered serious limitations. A more promising site was discovered by following a river upstream for fifteen miles, where Parramatta was founded. The river route between the two settlements was favoured for decades, until a road was built through the bush. Developments in territory beyond Sydney were encouraged by grants of land to free settlers.

James Brindley Bettington arrived in New South Wales in 1827 and was soon in a position to begin business in wool by acquiring a wharf at Darling Harbour, in the heart of Sydney. It seems the venture was well planned in advance, for a published report suggests that his father's firm in London had applied for a grant of land. The young man's interest in breeding sheep led him to Parramatta and the land beyond, where he quickly took part in the agriculture and associated business of the colony.

James Brindley Bettington must have inherited some of the qualities of his grandfather; both had the courage and confidence to develop new ground while setting high standards. The young man gained awards for his breeding of sheep and horses in the newly settled country and he had the enterprise and business sense to establish trade and manage land. Eventually he was involved in the farming of a vast acreage through grant, purchase and lease in several places. In 1850, for example, there was a lease of 90,000 acres and before the turn of the century the canal engineer's great-grandson, also named James Brindley Bettington, was able to farm 58,000 sheep on the family's estate of Brindley Park. The interests of the first James Brindley Bettington extended to local and state government during the early years of New South Wales and upon his death in Plymouth, England, he was described as a landed proprietor of Parramatta. There were Bettington relatives in Bath, England.

The rearing of sheep and horses and trading in wool was reminiscent of the farming activities of Brindley's Bowman relatives in Derbyshire, over a century earlier, but the scale of the enterprise would have amazed the villagers where the young James Brindley had tended his father's animals in the hills above Buxton. However, thousands of acres of New South Wales were often brown and parched through heat and drought, so that several acres were required to support each sheep.

The marriage of James Brindley Bettington in 1830 provides a further point of interest in Brindley's history, for the bride was Rebecca, a daughter of William

Lawson, one of the three explorers famous for their discovery of a passage through the Blue Mountains of New South Wales in 1813. Another of the trio was William Wentworth, who in 1852 founded the University of Sydney.

It had been vital to overcome the obstacle of the Blue Mountains, as new pastures were required urgently for the expanding flocks of animals in the region of Sydney and Parramatta. No one knew what lay beyond the mountains, but there was also a demand for fresh food from the rapidly increasing population of Sydney. The Blue Mountains hemmed in the coastal strip of land and appeared to be an insurmountable barrier, with sheer cliffs, ravines, waterfalls and a dense growth of brush and eucalyptus, known as blue gum trees. The mountain range had acquired its name because the evaporation of droplets of eucalyptus oil appears as a blue haze from a distance. Previous attempts to penetrate the obstacles had failed, but Blaxland, Lawson and Wentworth took four servants, all ex-convicts, four horses and five dogs. They made slow progress hacking a way through and taking horses on difficult climbs. Twenty-six days later, the party returned home exhausted, ill and short of supplies, but convinced that they had seen plains of grazing land from a high point. Close by, three peaks were named Mount Blaxland, Lawson's Sugar Loaf and Wentworth's Sugar Loaf. However, historians are unable to confirm whether Blaxland or Lawson took the important decision to find a route along the mountain ridges rather than by descent into deep, rock strewn valleys. On 14 February 1814, the Governor of the colony rewarded each of the three men with a gift of 1,000 acres of land. William Lawson's Journal is on microfilm in the Mitchell Library, Sydney, and an 'Explorers' Tree', marked by the three men in 1813, is at the side of the road to Bathurst.

In 1800, Lawson had gone to Australia as a soldier of the New South Wales Corps, initially being stationed on the penal colony of Norfolk Island, 800 miles off shore and noted for its inaccessible cliffs. Later, Lt William Lawson's service in Sydney resulted in his return to England for the court martial of Major Johnston of the 'Rum Corps', a reference to the regiment's dealing in the liquor. The major had led an attempt at rebellion against Governor Bligh, of the famous *Bounty* mutiny. Lawson had first hand knowledge of the events and people, but his wife was in Australia and he sailed for Sydney before giving evidence.

By 1819 Lawson was Commandant of Bathurst, a troop station beyond the Blue Mountains. There he occupied a Government building and he already had a farm at Prospect, near Parramatta. A considerate man, Lawson served in the New South Wales Veterans' Company and acquired a grant of land from Governor Macquarie. He built a mansion for himself and called it 'Veteran Hall', which became the birthplace of James Brindley's great-grandson, named after his father, James Brindley Bettington. More great-grandchildren of James Brindley followed and John Ward, in *The History of the Borough of Stoke upon Trent* (1843) named Anne, Rebecca and James - all Christian names being followed by 'Brindley Bettington'.

Grandfather William Lawson became one of the country's largest landowners; at one time his purchased and leased land totalled over 200,000 acres, with vast numbers of animals. He made further valuable explorations, served as a magistrate and was on the Legislative Council. Lawson and his associates appear in the

Australian Dictionary of Biography and his portrait is in the Mitchell Library, Sydney. With a place in New South Wales named Lawson and streets elsewhere bearing the name Bettington, it should be remembered that all Bettingtons were not descendants of James Brindley, as Susanna's widower, John Bettington, married for a second time.

Of the large family, William Lawson's two other sons-in-law, the brothers, Ambrose and Edward Hallen, should be mentioned, for Ambrose Hallen's daughter married her first cousin, the second James Brindley Bettington, their children being descendants of James Brindley, William Lawson, the Hallens and the Henshalls. Details of the Brindley Bettingtons and the architectural work of the Hallens are to be found in the *Australian Dictionary of Biography*. Edward Hallen designed the Sydney Grammar School, but returned to England for a time as an ironfounder in London, a fact which leads this researcher to wonder if there was a connection with the Hallen family of Lower Forge in Coalbrookdale in the previous century, especially as Ambrose and Edward had met Thomas Telford, the civil engineer engaged on work in Shropshire.

As there was no shortage of convict labour, the mountain road to Bathurst was soon laid sufficiently well for the troop station to be accessible. Travellers from overseas came to experience the 137 mile ride from Sydney into the interior and some wrote of the scenery, wildlife, wool carts, temperatures and the variable quality of the accommodation. In January 1836, nearly five years since leaving England, the Government survey ship, *The Beagle*, docked at Sydney. On board was the 27-year-old naturalist Charles Darwin, grandson of both Dr Erasmus Darwin and Josiah Wedgwood. Darwin spent over a week riding with a guide on the Blue Mountain road to Bathurst, making detours to view scenic wonders, flora and fauna. Initially, the bustling prosperity and social life of Sydney impressed him but before *The Beagle* set sail again Darwin had observed the divisions in the society, the excessive consumption of alcohol and large gangs of convicts in irons. Living conditions in the colony varied from large fenced houses to basic accommodation devoid of comfort. By this time Darwin was homesick and happy to leave.

At about the same period, Miss Anne Brindley, the canal engineer's elder daughter, travelled to Australia to visit her deceased sister's family. The length of her stay in New South Wales is not known but the voyage by sailing ship, via South Africa, took six months. In 1838, before she was able to tell her Staffordshire family of all she had seen, Anne died at sea during the return journey. Aged sixty-eight at her death, she had set out on quite an adventurous undertaking for an elderly spinster brought up far from the sea in industrial Longport and, unless she had made an initial trip to Liverpool at some time, Anne may not have known what to expect. Perhaps she had travelled with her younger nephew, John Henshall Bettington, to whom there is a brief reference in the *Australian Dictionary of Biography*. Her nephew's marriage at Bath in 1841 produced two daughters, and a descendant eventually published details of the pedigree and his inheritance of the few belongings of James Brindley (Campbell).

In 1817 the future of Miss Anne Brindley had been settled by the will of her Uncle Hugh Henshall, as unmarried ladies were provided for by the family in those days. Hugh Henshall left her his large house and estate at Greenway Bank, Norton-in-the-Moors, as long as she did not marry, but in the event of her marriage or death, the property was to pass to her half brother, Hugh Henshall Williamson. Although Anne was forty-seven years old, the will ensured that the property remained in the Henshall/Williamson family and Hugh Henshall Williamson was in residence before her death. In fact an agreement had been drawn up in which Miss Anne Brindley *'renounced her right'* to Greenway Bank and remained in Longport with her mother. The latter, as Brindley's widow, had renounced her rights in 1772, when her brother Hugh took over her affairs. One wonders if Anne junior received adequate compensation as her mother left the Longport house and potworks to Anne's half-sister, Catherine Williamson. HH Williamson was able to move into Greenway Bank immediately. He enlarged the estate and, being involved in a number of industrial concerns, served the County of Stafford, first as Deputy Sheriff and then as High Sheriff. Today Greenway Bank is a Country Park for the enjoyment of the people of the nearby City of Stoke-on-Trent.

In 1840, for some unknown reason, HH Williamson made a statement before the solicitor John Ward, declaring that he was brought up in the same household as his half-sisters, Anne and Susanna Brindley, and had papers to prove his mother was the widow of James Brindley, *'an eminent Engineer'*. He could prove that Anne and Susanna *'are the only issue of the said James Brindley and Anne his wife'*, and made reference to Susanna's descendants *'as I have been informed'*. It is strange that HH Williamson said the Brindley Bettingtons had gone to Van Dieman's Land (Tasmania) as Anne Brindley had died while returning from New South Wales only two years earlier. An advertisement in *The Staffordshire Advertiser* on 5 April 1834 described accommodation available on a ship sailing from Liverpool, calling at Van Dieman's Land (Hobart) and New South Wales (Sydney). Perhaps this added to Williamson's confusion. Although Anne Brindley may have travelled on a different ship at another time, the advertisement gives some idea of what she faced. This sailing ship was only three years old, was of 382 tons and could take a burthen of 600 tons. Nelson's *Victory* was over 2000 tons. Passengers in the small ship were assured of comfortable fittings, a well-aired atmosphere with seven feet between decks and the services of an experienced surgeon.

Most families pass on stories which may or may not be true, or have become distorted in the telling. On 6 June 1928, in the *Daily Express* newspaper, the novelist Arnold Bennett revealed his possible illegitimate descent from James Brindley. Subsequently, the baptism of an illegitimate John Bennett born to a Mary Bennett in Burslem, was found in the register for 1760, but there is unlikely to be proof of paternity after the passing of two centuries. Even Arnold Bennett, whose books sometimes featured his native Hanley and Burslem, mentioned the inference with caution, adding, *'with what truth I know not'*.

The tomb of Josiah
Spode III, son-in-law of
Ann Williamson,
formerly Brindley

Spode graves in Stoke
churchyard

CHAPTER 6
THE WIDOW AND THE WILLIAMSONS

James Brindley's premature death occurred in the early days of the period now referred to as the Industrial Revolution, before canal building brought 'The Canal Age' and before engines reached their full potential. However, the sons of Brindley's widow, from her subsequent marriage to Robert Williamson, were well positioned to take full advantage of the development of commerce, pottery and the heavy industries of coal mines and ironworks in North Staffordshire. Their success led to expansion, the absorption of smaller concerns and the ownership of terraced houses for workers in the hamlets around Tunstall.

Robert Williamson had left an estate of £5000, his pottery at Longport was well established and he and his family had associated with the leading potters and businessmen of the district. John Davenport and servants signed Robert's will. John Davenport was a skilled potter and it was thought that he moved into John Brindley's Longport works, but John Brindley left his property to members of his own family. Davenport made a porcelain service for the Coronation banquet of William IV.

On 16 November 1816, Hugh Henshall was buried at Newchapel, at the age of eighty-two. He had been a loyal and supportive brother to the twice widowed Ann Williamson. As a young surveyor, he had followed his father's profession, but was trained in canal engineering by James Brindley. After the death of Brindley, Hugh Henshall was given the responsibility of completing the Trent and Mersey Canal for the final five years of its construction. His epitaph reads:

HUGH HENSHALL ESQ
of the Firm of Hugh Henshall and Company
of the Trent & Mersey Canel
Late of Longport
departed this life
November 16 1816
in the 82 Year of his Age

Of interest is the spelling of 'Canel' which echoes that on the early map of the Duke of Bridgewater's canal, reproduced in Dr Boucher's biography of Brindley.

A copy of Hugh Henshall's will, on which probate was granted on 10 June 1817, covers 28 pages, for he had extensive properties in Longport and in Cheshire. His bequests to Brindley's grandsons, then young men in their early twenties, have been referred to here earlier and likewise provision for his niece Miss Anne Brindley at Greenway Bank. Hugh Henshall had also provided for young Robert Williamson in 1809, with a marriage settlement of an *'estate, farms, mines and premises'* at Goldenhill and Ranscliff, near Tunstall. Robert's bride was Anne Kinnersley, the daughter of Thomas Kinnersley, a banker of Newcastle-under-Lyme, who eventually bought the Clough Hall estate from John Gilbert's son. Thomas Kinnersley's son succeeded him there and, like the Williamsons, owned coalmines and ironworks. The Henshall properties at Longport included potworks, crateworks, the Packhorse Inn and premises associated with the canal company and the Hendra Company, which brought clay from Cornwall. There were mining concerns in other places and a lime works at Newbold Astbury, not far from Ramsdell Hall in Cheshire where Robert Williamson went to live, free from industrial grime but facing the Macclesfield Canal.

John Ward's account of Tunstall and the surrounding hamlets makes numerous references to the industrial possessions of the Williamsons and the Kinnersleys. In Oldcott, which includes Goldenhill, Robert Williamson '...*works extensively the local mines on his own and neighbouring land, partly for supplying the Tunstall Potteries; but principally for the distant markets; whither they go by the Canal, to which he has a Railway, and an underground Branch Canal into the old Harecastle Tunnel; he likewise raises considerable quantities of ironstone, which is first calcined, and then forwarded for smelting, to South Staffordshire and Wales*'. The railway has also been described as a tramroad between the colliery and a wharf at the side of the Macclesfield Canal. It was conveniently close to Ramsdell Hall. Ward refers to a disused blast furnace in Oldcot and several blast furnaces operated by Thomas Kinnersley for the smelting of iron ore '*with which the neighbourhood abounds*'. Thomas Kinnersley of Clough Hall built an elegant church for himself and his numerous tenants, as well as a Sunday School for 500 children. Set in peaceful woodland, a short distance from his home, it provided, according to Ward, '...*one of the most lovely contrasts to the murky confines of Kidcrew* [Kidsgrove], *enveloped in continual smoke, that can possibly be imagined*'. Robert Williamson's son of the same name continued the family industry and by 1854 lived at Lawton Hall. Anne Williamson, nee Kinnersley, of Ramsdell Hall and the wife of Robert Williamson II, was buried alongside the Williamsons at Newchapel, in 1842.

John Henshall Williamson, another son of Brindley's widow, met a sad end in 1810. He enjoyed hunting, fishing, and sport, but drowned while swimming in the local Knypersey Pool with a young man of the Adams pottery family. Aged twenty-three, John was buried with his father at Newchapel.

Hugh Henshall Williamson of Greenway Bank, as mentioned previously, was also in industry and property, becoming High Sheriff by 1834, the year after Thomas Kinnersley held the position. HH Williamson married his second cousin, Anne Clowes, the daughter of William Clowes, a potter living in Porthill House. William's mother was Jane Henshall before marriage and William was also a nephew of Josiah Clowes, a canal and tunnelling engineer mentioned here earlier. Porthill was then a rural estate on top of the hill to Wolstanton and away from the smoke of Longport potteries. The Rogers, close relatives of John Brindley, were neighbours at The Watlands, Porthill.

St Anne's Church, Brown Edge has the Williamson coat-of-arms on its wall, HH Williamson having paid for the tower, spire and bells and much else. In 1844, the church was consecrated and the Bishop of Lichfield stayed with the Williamsons at Greenway Bank. In 1856, HH Williamson built a new road to the church for his coach and horses, creating New Lane and Old Lane. The church had a caretaker's house, stables and a coach house. HH Williamson died in 1867, aged 84 years.

There must have been some confusion. Four ladies of the Brindley/Williamson family were named Ann(e), with variable spelling. Miss Ann(e) Brindley was the daughter of Mrs Ann(e) Brindley, who became Mrs Ann(e) Williamson. Both daughters-in-law of the latter were named Mrs Anne Williamson.

Brindley's widow remained at Longport until her death. She was buried in the same grave as her second husband, her drowned son and her dear brother; in the next grave but one to James Brindley at Newchapel. The inscription reads:

Ann

Relict of the aforesaid Robert Williamson

departed this Sepr 26th 1826 Aged 79 Years

Ann died one day short of 54 years after the death of Brindley. John Ward wrote, *'We may truly add, respecting this excellent lady, that her memory will be long cherished and revered, for her extensive beneficence and goodness'*. Ann left her Longport property, house and potworks, to her unmarried daughter, Catherine Williamson, who was buried at Newchapel in 1853.

The other Williamson daughters married well. Jane's husband was John Robinson MD; Elizabeth married into the Boyes family and had several children, while Mary married Josiah Spode III, executor of the will of his mother-in-law. His father was Josiah Spode II, who had greatly improved the pottery of Josiah Spode I and expanded the works close to the Trent and Mersey Canal at Stoke. He was noted especially for producing bone china and vast quantities of the popular blue printed ware. The Spode factory was visited by the Royal Princes, later George IV and William IV, and Spode was 'appointed' royal potter during their reigns. He became one of the wealthiest men in the district and built a mansion called 'The Mount'. The estate of 150 acres was on the hill at Penkhull, looking towards the moorland beyond Stoke. The Hartshill portion of this land later became the site of the new North Staffordshire Infirmary when it moved from Etruria. The Prince of Wales laid the foundation stone in 1866. From 1891 the Mount itself became the North Staffordshire Institute for the Deaf and Blind

Mary Spode's husband was a churchwarden at Stoke, when he, his father and others laid foundation tablets for a new Parish Church in 1826. The tablets incorporated samples of Spode products, Josiah II having contributed a large sum of money towards the building. He died in 1827, before the church was complete. His memorial, like that of Josiah Wedgwood, is in Stoke Church and both are buried in the churchyard. The Spode family tombs are in a corner, while the church holds memorials to two sons-in-law of Mrs Ann Williamson - a wall plaque to John Robinson and a sculpture of a weeping woman in memory of Josiah Spode III above the heraldic arms of Spode and Williamson impaled. Simeon Shaw valued his friendship with Mary's husband, Josiah III, and described him as being *'unaffected by the caprices of fortune'*, and one who gave aid to the *'suffering Poor'*. Within two years of his father's death, Josiah Spode III died quite suddenly at the age of fifty-two, leaving Mary with their six-year-old son at The Mount. Mary and young Josiah IV moved for the benefit of his education and he attended Trinity College, Cambridge, for one year and the Inner Temple, London, briefly. A grandson of Brindley's widow by her second husband, he settled at Armitage Park in south east Staffordshire, becoming a JP and then High Sheriff of the county by 1850.

Mary Spode lived nearby at Brereton Lodge and left a simple will, an estate of £600, £10 gold remembrance rings for her close family and some personal belongings to her daughter-in-law. Her son was not connected with the pottery trade of his ancestors and he filled his house with architectural treasures. A childless widower, he became a Roman Catholic and founded Hawkesyard Priory in his castellated and pinnacled mansion, part of which is now known as the Spode Conference Centre on a busy road out of Rugeley.

The coal and iron industries of the Williamsons continued until the 1880s when troubles brought court cases and bankruptcy. Large numbers of workmen were unemployed and there was hardship for their families; not unusual at that period.

The North Staffordshire Infirmary built on land that was part of the Mount estate

The Mount later became the North Staffordshire Institution for the Deaf and Blind

CHAPTER 7
BRINDLEY BROTHERS

James Brindley's parents lived long enough to be aware of their son's fame and knew something of the prosperity of his brothers, who began work before the period of greatest industrial change. The nature of relationships within the family is not known, James noted a payment to his brother-in-law, Samuel Simcock, but Samuel was a trusted assistant. Despite James Brindley's apparently strong physique, he died decades before his brothers and they, having descendants, had no need to mention each other in wills. Joseph Brindley became a millwright and leased the Smelting Mill at Alton, firstly through the Gilberts and then from the Earl of Shrewsbury. In 1790, Joseph made a brief reference to his youngest brother, Henry and his sister Ann Allen concerning his property. John Brindley became a potter of some standing, built the first factory at Longport and retired to Union Hall, Kinver. Henry was the miller at Danebridge Mill (Staffs), with connections in Wincle, Bosley and Gawsworth (Ches). In the 19th century, Henry's son and grandson became millers at the Mill Street premises in Leek, while the first wife of the said grandson was a great-grand-daughter of Joseph Brindley of Alton. Previously, a grandson of Joseph had married a grand-daughter of John Brindley of Kinver. Such intermarriage was common, especially when there was property, even leased property, to be retained in the family unit.

JOHN BRINDLEY

John Brindley, the third son, was the brother most closely associated with James, as John had an interest in improving transport. He served on the committee of the Trent and Mersey Canal and was regarded by Meteyard as one of the more practical members, able to *'second the plans and suggestions of their great engineer'*, with John Gilbert and Samuel Garbett, a chemical manufacturer in Birmingham and Scotland.

In 1730, when John Brindley was about ten years old, he was sent to Burslem to learn the art and skill of potting, according to the Adams family of potters. At the time of Josiah Wedgwood's birth, young John was already receiving instruction. He must have been offered the opportunity as a consequence of close ties between the people of Leek and Burslem, the pottery town which stands high and exposed on the fringe of the moorlands. Early in the 18th century, it was a small village with grass, trees and subsistence farming, enabling inhabitants to provide just enough fresh food to accompany their staple diet of oats in the form of oatcakes. Made from oat batter poured onto a hotplate, or bakestone, the substantial and pliant discs are popular served with butter or hot cheese and bacon. Moorland places remained rural and remote, but the ancient parish of Burslem and neighbouring settlements contained clay, coal and iron. The expansion of industry from these resources ruined the rural atmosphere and gave birth to the unique landscape of the City of Stoke-on-Trent, of which Burslem is a constituent town with Tunstall, Hanley, Stoke, Fenton and Longton - six towns together.

Long before the pottery industry developed fully, smallholders found their

A view of Alton and the castle
c1800

Josiah Wedgwood's Ivy
House works in Burslem

The Trent and Mersey Canal at Longport (1992)

smooth, paste-like clay could be formed into pots and bricks which, after drying were 'fired', or baked. They helped themselves to clay from waste land or even from holes in muddy tracks, and built low, round 'kilns' or ovens on their holdings for the firing of coarse brown pots. Many of these were butter pots for farmers on richer pastures to the south of the area. Most potting families had a small workshop and kiln along with a few animals. Gradually, all kinds of improvements were discovered by trial and error over the centuries. Brown clays, white clays, additions to clay, the temperatures of the firings, the number of firings, decorations, glazes, moulds and a wider range of products were to be considered and developed. Improvements in transport became essential for the clay and materials, as well as for the manufactured goods.

John Brindley acquired considerable skill at his craft and became a 'Master Potter'. He set up his own works in Burslem and produced a high standard of ware, enabling him to take an apprentice at a time when it was customary for potters to send their sons to be trained by other local potters. In 1756, William Adams of Greengates was placed with John Brindley and the view that Adams trained with Josiah Wedgwood has been corrected by PWL Adams.

In 1748, John Brindley married Ann, the daughter of Francis Rogers, a Burslem potter. (There was a Francis Rogers in Burslem in the previous century). Ann's brother, also Francis, had property in Mill Street, Leek. By his will, his three orphaned children, two boys and a girl, were placed in the guardianship of John Brindley. The brothers, John and George Rogers, became well-known potters in their own right. John Brindley's first wife died long before her brother and, although several children of John and Ann Brindley were baptised, James, a potter, was the only one mentioned in his will. Although James died before his father, it seems that he was the only one to have survived long enough to produce heirs to their grandfather's business interests.

John Brindley became a widower in September 1758 and married again in September 1760, when he took time away from his pottery to apply for a marriage by licence at Stoke Church, where he and Hannah Stevenson, née Taylor, were married that same day. The couple travelled three miles to the church as marriage by licence in a neighbouring parish gave a little privacy from friends and employees. Banns were not called, an extra fee was charged and some status was added to the proceedings on a special day out.

As mentioned in Chapter 3, it may have been only coincidental that in 1760, a house, work premises, an oven and land at Goldenhill were, or had been lately, in the tenure of John Taylor, a potter, and yet John Brindley was soon involved in the partnership there. The area, which included Goldenhill and Turnhurst, was known to be rich in minerals and the family names of tenants had changed little from the previous century. Robert Hurst, the Gilbert's relative, purchased the whole estate four months before John and Hannah Brindley's wedding, but the estate was to be divided into four shares. In 1760 Longbridge, two miles southward, was the northern limit of James Brindley's canal plan for Staffordshire, while the Duke of Bridgewater's Canal into Worsley mine was still under construction. In 1808, John Brindley's will bequeathed a house and *'premises'* at Goldenhill to his youngest grandson, Thomas John Brindley, without reference to mining or a branch canal into Harecastle.

As a young woman Hannah Taylor had married Thomas Stevenson, a Burslem potter. Adding weight to the idea that John's second wife was connected with Goldenhill/Newchapel is the fact that the marriage was at the parish church in Wolstanton. Thomas Stevenson died intestate in 1757 and any surviving children have not been researched here. Hannah signed probate documents which provide an insight into the premises of an individual potter before mechanisation.

The Stevensons' home had been simply furnished with household goods worth £52 in a large parlour, two chambers above, a little parlour, a kitchen and a cellar. There was a furnace and utensils such as tubs, pans, bottles and a bottle rack, a sieve and stools. The house had chairs, a clock, pewter weights, a chest and surprisingly, six pictures worth 1s 6d. Pictures rarely appeared in local inventories. Thomas left little money and few clothes, but he kept a cow, a small rick of oats, a small *'parcel of hay'*, a churn and a milking pail. His pottery had a warehouse, a workhouse and an oven, with a lathe wheel and a saggar wheel. Wooden boards were for easing the carriage of the newly-formed pots, while iron ones were used in the intense heat of the oven. Pottery saggars, or containers, held the ware in the oven. Close at hand were tongs, iron ladles, shovels and a poker. The workhouse had a paddle for mixing the glaze, fine sieves of lawn and hair, with a 'glosing ladder' and a bag of salt for use in the glazing process. Salt glazing took place during the second firing, when the oven reached a certain high temperature and the salt was shovelled into the furnace causing vapours to form an impervious glaze on the surface of pots. The 'scaffold' was for reaching the top of the kiln and the salt was dropped through the hole in the top of the dome - a gaseous process which, with the hazard of dust from the clay, may have contributed to Thomas's early death. He employed an assistant or an apprentice, as his working area had two tables, two stools and a trestle. Stored materials were *'about 50 load of clay in Burslem'*, and a similar load in a field, flints, some unfired ware and Cheshire clay. The latter was brought as large balls in panniers on mules along the rutted tracks of the unmade roads.

John and Hannah Brindley settled to married life anew, having two children. Susanna, named after her grandmother of Lowe Hill, only lived for two years, while a son, Taylor Brindley, died in 1786, aged twenty-three. In 1788 his father signed probate papers, Taylor having been in possession of a pottery in Fenton and being included in a list of potters with manufacturers such as Clowes and Williamson.

It was fortunate that Taylor Brindley's mother did not know of his death; she had been keen to perpetuate her maiden name, but motherhood brought her great sadness. John Brindley had been a widower again since July 1779, shortly before the death of his mother at Lowe Hill, but his wife had been able to enjoy a few years in the large house built for John next to his new canalside works at Longport. PWL Adams described the house as *'substantial'*, in the style of the Queen Anne period, three storeys high and facing Trubshaw Cross at the junction of roads to Burslem, Tunstall and Newcastle-under-Lyme. Longport is near to Longbridge Hayes and was originally called Longbridge, where a long bridge of planks crossed the Fowlea Brook and surrounding marsh. Longport came into being through the construction of the Trent and Mersey Canal and John Brindley, the first manufacturer to build premises there, must have planned the development long before his brother's death. John, a shareholder and committee member would be able to receive loads of clay and other materials by boat and, like Josiah Wedgwood, be more certain that large quantities of pottery were carried with fewer breakages.

Josiah Wedgwood's new factory by the canal was less than a mile from Longport, nearer to Stoke. His new mansion, pottery and houses for the workers was called Etruria, but this 'new' word caused John Brindley and probably many others, a little difficulty with the spelling. Even Wedgwood sometimes began it with an 'H'. Although serving on the same committee, John Brindley annoyed Wedgwood by objecting to the course of the canal in front of Wedgwood's Etruria Hall. John and others thought that Wedgwood had been favoured to provide a better view, but Wedgwood wrote to Thomas Bentley, *'Mr Brindley's brother is at the head of this affair'*, and knowing *'Brindley the Great to be an honest man'*, recalled him to check the survey. James presented his unaltered opinion at the next Committee meeting at Trentham. How this affected the relationship between the Brindley brothers is not known. Probably, both were far too busy to be unduly troubled. It was just part of business life.

Meteyard quoted a letter of 1765, in which Wedgwood wrote to Bentley, *'The Duke of Bridgewater lay at Trentham on Wednesday evening on his way to London, & sent for Mr John Brindley & me to attend him there. We had the honour to sup, breakfast & spend about eight hours with his Grace. The subject you may be sure was inland Navigation... Mr John Gilbert* (his steward of the works) *was present ...On Saturday Mr John Gilbert was sent to Burslem to us to give us some further hints, instructions & encouragmt, in our design.'* And so the Duke knew both Brindley brothers.

The Wedgwood collection of invoices show that John Brindley's pottery was known for high standards of production and met Wedgwood's requirements by supplying Thomas Wedgwood of *'A Truray* [Etruria]' with large quantities of ware, presumably to make up an order, which was not an unusual arrangement between potters. Some manufacturers would buy good plain ware for decoration at their own premises. An invoice of 20 April 1768 records that John Brindley supplied Mr *'Joseah'* Wedgwood with dozens of dishes and plates in the *'Inday'* [India?] pattern in different sizes at a cost of over £17.

The working relationship between John and the Wedgwoods continued, John writing a letter on 18 May 1787 headed *'Mr Thomas Wadgwood* [sic]. *Bot* [Bought] *of John Brindley'*. It is well written, accompanies neat, well-kept accounts and reads:

Sr.
I have Not tacken Discount of but wil tackit of in the Naxt bill I shal be glad to see You to morrow & youer Son
I am youer Varey Huml. Sirt.
    John Brindley

Of course, John Brindley's spelling reflects the manner of speech in the area and few of the inhabitants met people from outside their remote district. 'Tackit' for 'take it' is exactly as it is often said. 'Your very humble servant' was a standard ending to a letter in those times and John Brindley was no humble servant.

John Brindley's letter

In 1773, Josiah Wedgwood received an order which he described as the 'Execution of the noblest plan ever laid down, or undertaken by any manufacturer in Great Britain'. He was commissioned to make a huge service in creamware for the Empress of Russia, Catherine the Great, who wished each piece to be unique with the decoration of a different English view for over 900 pieces. Wedgwood included views of the estates of Staffordshire noblemen, such as Earl Gower and the Earl of Stamford, who provided valuable assistance. In 1776, Wedgwood dined with the helpful Lord Stamford and his brother at Trentham Hall, the home of Earl Gower, the brother-in-law of the Duke of Bridgewater. The noblemen, Wedgwood and the two Brindleys, knew or knew of each other through pottery and canal business. Nearly twenty years later, for some unknown reason, John Brindley, in retirement, became a neighbour of the Earl of Stamford in the south of the county.

The Brindleys and Henshalls naturally knew many potters and people in allied trades. John Shrigley, who was associated with James Brindley on the 1760 map of the proposed Staffordshire Canal, had a son-in-law named Daniel Morris, a maltster of Church Lawton, in Cheshire. John Brindley's son and heir, named James Brindley, a potter of Burslem, married Catharine [sic] Morris of Lawton in April 1784. Witnesses to the ceremony were John Morris, Daniel Morris and the bridegroom's cousin, John Rogers of Longport. There may have been more than one Daniel Morris as Wedgwood's letters refer to a Daniel Morris of Lawton, the trusted carrier of his letters, crates of ware, moulds, clay and even drawings, when transport was a string of mules. Morris of Lawton was the first carrier to use carts when the condition of the roads began to improve. In 1771, John Brindley was actively interested in the development of roads, signed with famous potters at a meeting of the Trustees of the Turnpike Roads from Lawton to Burslem and Newcastle-under-Lyme, and provided a toll house at Longport.

John's son, James, died in 1795 at the age of 41 years, leaving Catharine and several children. One of their sons had lived for three months, while another of ten years had been afflicted by pain for a long period and died a month after his father. In the same year Catharine gave birth to Thomas John Brindley, but he was not baptised until 1806, in Kinver Parish Church; surely a sign that his mother took a long time to overcome her losses. She had a daughter, also named Catharine, and four sons - James, Joseph, William and Thomas John, heirs to their grandfather's various properties and taken to live with him at Kinver.

John Gilbert and Josiah Wedgwood also died in 1795 and it was during that distressful year that old John Brindley arranged to live forty miles away in Kinver. In 1795, a deed between John Brindley and William Hodgetts Esq enabled John Brindley to settle in the recently built Union Hall, on the outskirts of Kinver and bordering the Earl of Stamford's estate of Enville Hall. The owner of Union Hall had suffered a fatal riding accident on Kinver Edge and his heir preferred to live elsewhere. Decades earlier the landowners affected by the building of the Staffordshire and Worcestershire Canal and the Earl may have provided accommodation for the engineer as did the Duke of Bridgewater at Worsley. Some confusion has arisen due to the fact that there had been a George Brindley at the Hyde Mill, a slitting mill at Kinver, nearly 200 years before. Over the centuries, these earlier Brindleys, also said to have roots in Leek, married with the Foleys and the Foleys married Hodgetts, both landed families with property in north and south Staffordshire. However, the early Brindleys in Kinver ceased to appear in the register there in the first part of the 18th century.

John Brindley's interest in business did not decrease with age and in 1805 he became the owner of an ironworks at Brockmoor, a few miles from Kinver. In 1805, he probably arranged the marriage of his 16 year-old grand-daughter, Catharine Brindley of Kinver, to 30 year-old Joseph Brindley, grandson of his deceased brother, Joseph Brindley of the Smelting Mill at Alton. The second cousins were married by licence in Kinver and returned to live at Longport, where Joseph, a 'gentleman', was a lime master and Secretary of the Hendra Company, which brought supplies of white clay from Cornwall, via Liverpool and the Trent and Mersey Canal.

John Brindley (d1807) was about 88 years old at his death (80yrs on his gravestone) and described as a 'gentleman' in his long, but uncomplicated will. His widowed daughter-in-law, Catharine, nee Morris, received an annuity as there were no pensions in those days. Her daughter, also named Catharine, was left £100 so soon after her marriage settlement. Grandson James Brindley, an executor of the will at 22 years of age, received the property *'near Compton and Kinver Edge'*, with land at Longport and Wolstanton and more property at Longport in the possession of William Clowes and Hugh Henshall. Grandson Joseph inherited property in Kinver held under lease and became known as Joseph Brindley of Union Hall, although the property was known as Brindley Hall for a time. The Brockmoor ironworks were to be sold and the proceeds divided between James and Joseph. The property at Great Chell, in Wolstanton parish, was for the third grandson, William, and it was to provide the annuity for his mother. William was also to have buildings and property at Longport occupied by John Rogers and his undertenants, shops, works and a public house. The youngest grandson, Thomas John, was left the house and buildings at Goldenhill, property built by his father at Longport and a piece of land which had been leased to Robert Williamson II. John Davenport, a Longport potter, was not mentioned.

In Kinver churchyard, the tomb of John Brindley and his family is beginning to crumble inside its railings. The view from the site looks beyond the village towards the

house where John Brindley retired 200 years ago. His descendants bought more land from the Earl of Stamford and sold land for the old school, which is now the village library. There is a Brindley Heath and Brindley Heath Junior School - but the name may have come from the Old English for a 'burnt clearing', from the Brindleys at Hyde Mill in the 17th century, or from the 19th century Brindleys.

Succeeded by four grandsons and a grand-daughter, John Brindley might have expected many male heirs in the next generation. However, his grand-daughter Catharine produced six daughters and

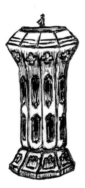

The font and lantern in
Kinver Church

The tomb of John Brindley and his family at Kinver, Staffs

one son from her marriage to her second cousin. Grandson James died childless. Grandson Thomas John, it seems, did not marry (d1848, aged 53 yrs). Grandson William left two daughters and one son. Grandson Joseph of Union Hall had a son and a daughter, neither married and both predeceased their parents. The son had trained as a barrister. John Brindley's great grand-daughters married professional men out of the district. The two great-grandsons - John and John James Brindley - have not been researched further.

When Joseph Brindley of Union Hall died in 1863, he expressed a wish for '*...ornate windows Tastefully painted or stained Glass ...in memory of myself and the other in memory of my wife*', in Kinver Church. In recent years the church required extensive repairs and the Brindley windows were removed. In keeping with the rebuilding, a modern lantern has been made from a Brindley window and another belonging to the Price family. The splendid Price-Brindley lantern hangs over the font, and illumination shows the full radiance of the Victorian glass. It records the deaths of Catharine, with Caroline and Joseph Pargeter Brindley, the latter two being the adult children of Joseph and Caroline Brindley of Union Hall, as mentioned above.

Mrs Caroline Brindley, Joseph's widow, was left to arrange the making of the window and the maintenance of the Brindley tomb in Kinver. Her investment for the latter was recorded on a large board above the south aisle of the church in 1885. Any residue was for the poor and aged widows of the parish.

Surviving letters mention that Joseph Brindley of Union Hall received a grant of arms about 1850. Sleigh's *History of the Ancient Parish of Leek* (2nd ed. 1883) reproduced an heraldic shield for the Brindley line, with three scallops in the design. The descendants of James Brindley, the engineer, possess a fob seal bearing arms. It was made by Wedgwood and Bentley, who were using joint names on pottery in the period 1769-80.

It seems appropriate to mention John Brindley's relatives, the Rogers family, whose pottery is appreciated by collectors of antiques. John, George and Ann Rogers were in the guardianship of their Uncle John Brindley following the decease of their father. They were under eight years old and their Grandfather Rogers was aged and required care. Most likely John and George were trained in the pottery business by John Brindley. On reaching 21 years, they came into their inheritance from their father, Francis Rogers. John Rogers received the potworks and buildings, a silver tankard, a writing desk and £2000, a goodly sum to launch him into business. George

The Watlands, Porthill, home of Spencer Rogers

inherited a little silver and £300, while Ann was left a house in Burslem, £300, a silver sauceboat, cream jugs and spoons. The pottery works of the brothers began trade under the title 'John and George Rogers'.

John Brindley, as guardian, gave consent to the marriage of John Rogers and Margaret Spencer, who was the daughter of the vicar of Burslem. The young couple named their son Spencer Rogers. Sadly Margaret soon died. George Rogers married Harriet Smith in Stafford. They were childless and became legally separated. This left John's only son, Spencer Rogers, to inherit the business and property. George and John died in 1815 and 1816 respectively and the business continued as 'John Rogers and Son'. The family's servants were to be cared for and John left £1000 for the local infirmary as well as money to raise the ancient, small tower of Burslem Church so that it could take a set of bells, but the work was not done in the specified time. Spencer was sailing in the Mediterranean when he inherited £4000 and a gold watch from Uncle George Rogers. Spencer was described at the time as a merchant of Liverpool and Uncle George left him a share in a brig, a two-masted sailing ship called *Hero*. He may have supervised overseas trade and visited classical sites - the firm excelled in blue printed classical views with flowery borders, in designs such as 'ATHENS' and 'FLORENCE', while interest in the sea extended to a series of plates with a naval theme. The facility of the canal to the ports widened horizons well beyond the confines of North Staffordshire.

Spencer was an able potter and had inherited the recently built mansion called The Watlands or Watlands Hall, then set in parkland above Porthill, to the west of Longport and clear of the smoke from the pottery kilns. He lived with his elderly spinster Aunt Ann in *'the sweets of domiciliary quiet, after the fatigues of commercial activity'*, and was a neighbour of William Clowes of Porthill House, the father-in-law of Hugh Henshall Williamson of Greenway Bank. In 1831, Spencer Rogers held office as Chief Constable of Burslem. His aunt died in 1841 and Mr T Markin's research found that the pottery ceased to trade as Spencer was declared bankrupt in 1842. His business manager, Edward Cole, lived at Turnhurst with his family until 1841, when he lived next to Spencer Rogers' pottery, known as Dale Hall Pottery, at Longport. However, Spencer had financial difficulties over a long period, with bills unpaid in 1827 and a large mortgage arranged on houses he owned in 1834.

The Watlands was sold to Lewis Adams in 1842 and by 1843, Harriet, the estranged widow of George Rogers was in a debtors' prison, and making claims on her nephew, Spencer Rogers. This was a sad end to a successful pottery, whose wares can be seen in the Victoria and Albert Museum, London, and are valued by collectors.

JOSEPH BRINDLEY

Little is generally known of Joseph Brindley, a brother of the canal engineer and most likely next to him in age. He became a millwright and yet no record of his training or early work has been found so far. Only documents pertaining to his grandchildren confirm the fraternal relationship between the millwright of Alton and John Brindley of Kinver. Joseph had been named in the will of his father and that of his brother-in-law, William Allen, an innkeeper of Leek and Tittesworth, but neither gave a hint of Joseph's whereabouts or occupation.

The village of Alton is set above the steep-sided valley of the River Churnet, where its situation is particularly attractive, with wooded slopes, a castle and the former home and gardens of the Earls of Shrewsbury at Alton Towers. In Joseph Brindley's time, the castle was a ruin and the towers and gardens across the valley had not been created. Upstream from the village, the Brindleys lived at the Smelting Mill, which is

still marked as such on the Ordnance Survey map, although it became a corn mill over 200 years ago. It is now a ruin, with water pouring through a stationary wheel of rusting metal. The water from the mill pool was from Dimmingsdale, just before its confluence with the River Churnet, the river that worked James Brindley's mill in Leek. It is disappointing that no documents mention James and Joseph together in their working life.

A view of the remains of the Smelting Mill at Alton, Staffordshire

Joseph married Sarah Bennit/Bennett at Alton, by licence on 17 December 1746, aged 26 and 21 years respectively, according to the marriage bond. The bridegroom had the status of a yeoman of 'Cawdon' [Cauldon], a place known for its limestone quarries, of interest to the young John Gilbert. Joseph may have been at Caldon Mill on the River Hamps. It has been thought that Matthew was the first child of Joseph and Sarah Brindley, but recent research suggests that their first child was baptised James at Waterfall nearby, some months before Matthew was baptised at Alton Church. It was customary to name the first son after his paternal grandfather and the second son after his maternal grandfather, the latter being Matthew Bennett.

Joseph Brindley and his family moved to Checkley, where four daughters were baptised between 1751 and 1756. There were mills on the River Tean and, in 1747, a tape making factory was set up by the Philips family of Tean, in the parish of Checkley, but Joseph Brindley's place of work is unknown. Joseph's wife Sarah died in 1758, in the same year that ten-month old Joseph died. Joseph, the widower, married Lydia Lightwood at Alton Church in 1762. A son and daughter, Henry and Lydia, were born in quick succession, but their poor mother was buried in 1763, aged 45. Joseph needed a mother for his children and on 3 July 1764, at Leek and by licence, he married Mary Mobberley, a 50 year-old spinster from a family of small farmers at Bradnop, near Lowe Hill. She died in 1786.

At the time of the 1764 marriage, Joseph was described as a millwright and he already occupied the Smelting Mill at the entrance to the sylvan Dimmingsdale. The lead ore was brought from small mines in the surrounding moorlands and the water-power operated bellows in the smelting process. The mill was the property of the Earl of Shrewsbury and was leased to Thomas Gilbert of Cotton in 1747, when Gilbert was 26 years old and yet to become the agent of Earl Gower. Eventually, Thomas Gilbert sublet the mill to Joseph Brindley, but by 1786, the Earl's mill was leased directly to Joseph, who signed the document on which he was described as an 'Engineer'.

The Smelting Mill consisted of, '*All that new erected Building some time ago used for smelting Lead commonly called a Smelting Mill Refinery and Slag Hearth but lately converted into a corn mill with the buildings thereunto situate and being upon Alton Common ...now in possession of Joseph Brindley his assigns or undertenants'*. The Earl of Shrewsbury was to retain rights to minerals, hawking, hunting, fishing and to the timber of the woodland, which still surrounds the mill and pool. Joseph Brindley would receive a warning when the pool was to be drained '*for fishing'*, presumably for maintenance. The tithe map of 1843 shows the 'Ancient mill' was exempt from tithes and the property included the house, garden, mill and millcroft situated in twenty-eight acres.

In 1786, Joseph was again described as an engineer on a deed concerning Alkins' Cottage and the Alkins' children, but before the end of the year his daughter Sarah was married to Thomas Alkins, 'gentleman', son of the deceased innholder of the same name. Joseph Brindley had property in Mill Street, Leek, and a few days before his death in 1790, the draft of a deed was drawn up. The very untidy writing was not Joseph's own. It concerned seven tenants and acknowledged the sum of £560. Joseph held the premises in 'fee simple', which meant that he could dispose of them as he pleased. His property in Alton passed to his sons-in-law by his will, which he signed in a shaky hand just eight days before his burial on 26 December 1790. Joseph Brindley's worn gravestone in Alton churchyard describes him as having been in the possession of '*the knowledge thereof of mechanical things'*. His three wives are recorded there although they were not all buried in Alton.

The obituary notice in the *Gentleman's Magazine* (vol. 61) described Joseph as a '*great mechanik'* and in a similar publication as a '*Mechanician'*, and yet it is not known how he earned such a title. He was quite aged when the smelting mill was converted to a corn mill. Success gave Joseph Brindley 'gentleman' status in his will and an estate valued at not more than £3000 for probate purposes. The lease of a malt house at the Smelting Mill was to be shared by Matthew Brindley, Thomas Salt and Thomas Alkins, while the lease of the Smelting Mill itself was to pass to Joseph's eldest daughter, Elizabeth Salt, who had married Thomas Salt in 1771, at Alton Church. If Thomas Salt became a widower, the lease would be his as long as he did not remarry and there were further conditions for the Salt children. Mr Joseph Salt, named as the miller in deeds dated 1811 and 1822, married his cousin Margaret Brindley, daughter of Uncle Matthew Brindley, his mother's brother. Married by licence in 1816, the witnesses were Margaret's brother, John Brindley, Clerk to the Brassworks, and his wife Frances (nee Mellor). John held this responsible position at Oakamoor, in the parish of Cheadle, while his father, Matthew Brindley, was Clerk to the Works, or manager, of the Alton Wire Mill Company by the River Churnet, below the village. The Wire Mill had thrived for decades, but in 1790, the year of Joseph Brindley's death, an old works at Oakamoor was developed into a rolling and slitting mill. Situated a short distance upstream, it supplied the brass and copper for the Alton Wire Mill.

In 1777, Joseph Tideswell married Joseph Brindley's daughter Susannah. He was a brass roller at the time and eventually worked at the Oakamoor site which opened in 1790. The couple had a family and were buried in Alton.

In 1770, Matthew Brindley married Lydia Walker, the 'girl next door' living at the Shaw House, separated from the Smelting Mill by woods and steep slopes. Her father, William Walker, provided a marriage portion of £50. Unfortunately, the Bishop's Transcript of Alton Parish Register gives the inaccurate information that Matthew married a Lydia Brindley in 1782, but the Parish Register names the bridegroom as James Hamersley. This Lydia was most likely Matthew's half-sister.

Matthew was a young man when his famous Uncle James Brindley was at the busiest period of his life and there was probably little contact. The signatures 'Jos. Brindley' and 'Jas. Brindley' at Matthew's wedding must have been those of his father and elder brother. In 1800, when Matthew's son John was married, the bride and groom were a little under the age of 21 and required parental consent. This apparently minor record proved to be invaluable to this research, for it brought to light the information that Joseph Brindley of Longport was another son of Matthew and confirmed the link between the Alton, Burslem and Kinver Brindleys. Fortunately this young Joseph, grandson of Joseph of Alton, had a stylish signature, which he often underlined with a flourish practised many times. The brothers, John of Alton, Clerk of the Brass Works, and Joseph of Longport, Burslem, a lime master, were named together on John's marriage bond. In 1805, Joseph, aged 30 years, married his second cousin, young Catharine Brindley of Kinver.

The wire mill used the water-power of the River Churnet. Matthew Brindley, having a lifetime's experience of the natural water systems at Alton, was asked to give an opinion as to whether the proposed Uttoxeter Canal would affect the river at the mill. However, Matthew failed to respond, perhaps because the Earl of Shrewsbury was his landlord and objected to the plan in case this was so. In 1809, the Earl agreed to the construction as long as a new weir was built to raise the water level. At one time, Matthew leased three cottages from the Earl and situated on five acres of land on the road to Farley. The cottages were in a poor state of repair and Matthew was responsible for rebuilding them according to certain specifications, but with access to free timber.

Matthew's death was reported in the county newspaper of 22 April 1820, when his decease, at 71 years, was *'deservedly regretted by all who knew him'*. A memorial tablet is attached

Rollers at a wire-mill.

to the wall of the south aisle of Alton Church, and dedicated to Matthew and his wife, Lydia. She signed the probate documents, as Matthew was another Brindley who failed to make a will. His estate was under £450 and his son John, of Oakamoor, was described as a *'gentleman of Cheadle'*. John moved back to the Alton Wire Works, which had become part of the Cheadle Brass Company, but in the 1820s the company had problems which led to the closure of the works. It was a period when many businesses had troubles. The mill closed in 1828, but John Brindley attempted to continue in business of some kind. In 1830 the premises by Alton Bridge were extensive and included a dwelling house and buildings such as a pigsty, a cowhouse, a stable, an office and a 'back kitchen' detached from the house. The Earl of Shrewsbury retained a right of way to his nearby coal yard, but the Brindleys were at liberty to use the Earl's crane to load and unload *'goods, wares or merchandise'* at the side of the Uttoxeter Canal. The Brindleys would have witnessed the upheaval involved in constructing the waterways, and the Uttoxeter Canal was an extension of the Caldon Canal, where James Brindley had been surveying when he developed his final illness, decades earlier.

The wire mill premises would be repossessed by the Earl if '...*the said Joseph Brindley and John Brindley their executors administrators or assigns became Bankrupt or insolvent or unable to pay* '. The date 9 February 1834 turned out to be disastrous for John Brindley as his brother, Joseph Brindley of Longport, died at the age of 59 years, leaving a widow and several children. Joseph, in spite of his experience in business and his ability to write well, had not made a will. On 5 April 1834, *The Staffordshire Advertiser* carried a notice for those who owed money to Mr Joseph Brindley and they were requested to pay the administrators - one of whom was Spencer Rogers. A further message appeared on the 3 May, *'Longport Lime Kilns are now in full work and any quantity of lime may be had upon application'*. Meanwhile John Brindley was in serious financial trouble and an announcement of his bankruptcy was made on the 10 May. Described as a colour manufacturer, a dealer and a chapman, or trader, he was to appear before Commissioners on the 17 June at the Royal Oak, Cheadle. Colour manufacture was for the pottery industry and John may have had contacts through his brother. There was no unemployment benefit in those days and men took every opportunity to earn enough to keep a wife and family.

John and Frances Brindley had a very large family indeed and 16 children were baptised between 1801 and 1824 at Alton Parish Church, but at least three died in infancy. In 1841, John and Francis appeared on the census as the occupants of a smallholding of five acres belonging to the Rev Thomas Gilbert of Cotton Hall close by. He was the son of Thomas Gilbert, who had first leased the Smelting Mill to John Brindley's grandfather and, of course, he was a nephew of John Gilbert, the deceased agent of the also deceased Duke of Bridgewater.

John's brother, the late Joseph Brindley of Longport (1775-1834), was laid to rest in Burslem churchyard; his polished black tombstone bearing slightly inaccurate dates. He had been Secretary of the Hendra Company, which had storage places by the Trent and Mersey Canal at Longport. As a young man in 1799, Joseph added his easily recognisable signature to a company document along with those of such well-

Part of the disused lime-kilns at Froghall

Burslem churchyard and the grave of Joseph Brindley of Longport

known potters as William Adams and Thomas Minton, and he was to sign many more. A number of pottery manufacturers had joined together to bring stone and clay from Hendra Common, near St Austell, Cornwall, to Liverpool by ship and then on canal boats to Longport. The materials were stored there on land leased from Hugh Henshall, who had completed the construction of the canal long since.

The descendants of the canal engineer's brother Joseph Brindley and his first wife become too numerous to be detailed here. Matthew, for example, had nine children and many grandchildren. The marriage of Matthew's son Joseph of Longport, to his cousin Catharine of Kinver, has been dealt with, but there was another inter-family link concerning Henry Brindley, the youngest of the canal engineer's brothers. A grand-daughter of Joseph's daughter married Henry's grandson, who eventually operated the famous mill in Mill Street, Leek, where he brought up his first and second family together.

It came about in this way. Joseph Brindley, brother of the canal engineer, had four sons-in-law: Thomas Salt, later of the Smelting Mill; Joseph Tideswell, a brass roller; Thomas Alkins; and John Cope of Alton, shoemaker. The latter married Mary Brindley and was left property in Alton by his father-in-law. It included a blacksmith's shop. The couple had two daughters; Esther stayed at home and cared for her widowed father, but her sister Mary became the wife of Joseph Malkin and lived at Wildgoose House, next door to Lowe Hill Farm. Eventually, on 29 August 1829, the Malkins' daughter Ann married a young James Brindley, a miller in Leek. The ceremony was witnessed by his brother Henry, also a miller. James and Henry were grandsons of Henry and Betty Brindley of Cheshire; Ann Malkin was a great grand-daughter of Joseph Brindley of Alton. The newly weds settled at Ashenhurst Mill, on a stream feeding the River Churnet and close to Lowe Hill. They named their two sons, Joseph and James. Sadly, Ann died in 1835, but James Brindley, miller, married again and occupied the Mill Street premises. Mary Malkin left savings for her two grandsons, who lived at Leek Mill with their father, their stepmother, also named Ann, and several half-brothers and sisters.

It was hoped that more information could be found concerning Joseph Brindley, but the following events were most unexpected. In 1998, a party of people from the United States of America visited the Brindley Mill, in Leek. It was not their first visit; they had a genealogical interest in the name and had founded an association, the Brindley International Historical Foundation. Some asked if James Brindley of canal fame had worked on canal construction in America. It seemed a strange idea; James Brindley had no time to spare and it was said that he had refused a request to go to France. A few years ago, Mr G Brindley and researchers in the USA discovered that the James Brindley associated with early canals in that country was the elder son of Joseph and Sarah of Alton. When the couple were 'of Cawdon', a baby James was baptised 8 May 1748 at the nearby church of Waterfall, shortly before Matthew, who was baptised in Alton 30 October 1748. Consequently, it is difficult to know when James was born, inaccuracy of ages in records and on gravestones being common.

As mentioned in an earlier chapter, this recently discovered James Brindley, the nephew, was trained by his uncle in canal engineering. He must have signed 'Jas.

Brindley', with his father's 'Jos. Brindley' when they were witnesses at Matthew's wedding in 1770. By 1774, a couple of years after his uncle's death, young James, aged about 28 years, sailed for America. On 7 July 1774, *The Virginian Gazette* announced the arrival of a party of, *'about forty ingenious Mechanicks'* including James and his cousin Thomas Allen of Leek, son of William and Ann Allen (nee Brindley).

John Phillips, the author of *Inland Navigation* (1805), a surveyor and builder, visited America. His writings were valued as he had worked for James Brindley for a time, viewed canals in Europe and worked on canals in Russia. He fought in the American War of Independence, was taken prisoner and saw canals while on parole. Phillips' writings were criticised as he rarely mentioned engineers other than James Brindley and by that time there were several worthy of note. In 1779, Phillips complained that *'our best mechanics and artificers are enticed by large rewards to emigrate...'* The long, wide rivers of North America were navigable for hundreds of miles, but improvements were needed on certain stretches, such as where there were narrows, falls and rapids. A canal system would enable trade to flourish without *'the danger of the sea, or uncertainty of adverse winds,'* and the irrigation of lowlands would be improved for the development of agriculture. Phillips mentioned the schemes for the Susquehanna and Potomac rivers without detail.

Young James was soon to meet George Washington and their contact is shown in George Washington's Letter Book and Maryland State Papers (Gordon Brindley, 2002). Washington believed that Mr Brindley possessed *'more practical knowledge of Cuts and Locks for the improvement of inland navigation than any among us as he was an executive officer (he says) many years under his uncle in this particular business.'* At times George Washington and James Brindley were guests in their respective homes. In 1777, before the battle of Brandywine in the American revolt against taxation and the struggle for independence from Britain, George Washington paced the floor with a coffee cup in his hand, in James Brindley's house. James even joined the militia, finally rising to the rank of second lieutenant on the side of the colonists 1778-1781. He also married in that period.

During the 1780s and 1790s, James Brindley was the manager, or chief engineer, of canal projects on the Susquehanna River and consultant on other schemes involving the James and Potomac rivers. His advice was requested in the states of the early settlers on the east coast, including South Carolina. Large locks were a feature where rivers were obstructed by falls some miles apart. James died in 1820 leaving descendants.

George Washington became the first President of the United States of America in 1789, but resigned in 1791 and died in 1799, aged 67 years. Phillips declared, *'...the immortal Washington was the original father and promoter of these canals and improvements, and well did he deserve that admirable motto, - 'Twice the saviour of his country. After conducting her to liberty, he opened her the way to prosperity by new roads and canals, and varying the produce of agriculture.'*

The coal and iron industries of Pennsylvania were developed, but rivers were canalized and railways built to such an extent that the State was in debt by 1840.

HENRY BRINDLEY

Henry Brindley did not make a name for himself and it was not easy to locate him for this research. He had moved into a neighbouring county. As mentioned earlier, Danebridge Mill, on the Staffordshire/Cheshire border, may have been leased by James Brindley senior to enable his sons James, Joseph and Henry to build up a family

business. There was a corn mill, a paper mill and a disused fulling mill on the site in the wooded valley of the River Dane. Maybe the scattered population did not weave enough woollen fabric to support a fulling mill for cleaning and thickening the material. Perhaps Joseph left for Cauldon/Caldon quite soon, leaving Henry to be trained and supervised by James for the standard seven years apprenticeship.

Danebridge

If this was the case, Henry would have spent a fair amount of time alone as James's skills as a millwright took him over many square miles on horseback and it is not certain where James regarded as home. Danebridge was a remote place to return to at the end of the day in all weathers.

Henry remained at Danebridge, probably with some manual assistance as corn-milling and paper-making would have been too much for the young apprentice alone. There is the possibility that he was helped by his father, but James senior had been an agricultural worker in his youth. Guidance from James junior would have been irregular from 1750, when he established a workshop in Burslem, worked on the restoration of Leek Mill and became involved in the Wet Earth Colliery project at about the same time. By 11 Dec 1754, Henry had proved himself and, by lease and release, his father passed the Danebridge Mill property over to him, his youngest son, making reference to *'younger sons'*, presumably excluding James. By this time only the corn mill was operational and the paper and fulling mills were *'sites'*. The property, then out of the hands of James senior, would be excluded from *'dower rights'* for his wife Susanna at his death. 'Dower rights' provided a widow with one third of her husband's estate. The address of James senior was given as *'Meer Knowles'* (Mare Knowles), an isolated farm below the eastern slopes of Wincle Minn on the Cheshire side of the River Dane and two miles from Danebridge. Had James senior separated from his wife, had his temperament caused trouble, was he helping at Danebridge, or was there a family link with Mare Knowles at an earlier period? In 1763, James senior made his will at his marital home *'the Lowe'* in Leek leaving the farm there to Susanna and then to his eldest son, James. Henry would receive five shillings as he had already received his share.

All that is known of Henry comes from parish registers, wills and documents concerning the mill. A single example of his signature shows excellent handwriting. Maybe his father's leasing of the mill tied Henry to its business and gave him something to pass to his children. There was no need for him to move on and he associated closely with his wife's family in Bosley, Gawsworth, and Sutton. The village of Wincle was just over the nearby bridge.

Henry, at about 30 years of age, married Elizabeth/Betty Shaw on 2 December 1756 at Prestbury Church. The bridegroom was *'of Wincle'* and his bride *'of Sutton'*, the village where James Brindley had trained with Abraham Bennett. The couple soon had a family although some died in infancy. A son James and an unnamed *'child of Henry Brindley of Wincle'* were buried in Bosley in 1764 and 1772, respectively. Betty's father, Samuel Shaw, had been a churchwarden at Bosley for a time, but at his death he was *'of Sutton'* and the property was to be shared by his sons and Betty Brindley, his daughter. In 1762, Henry *'of Heaton'* had signed the probate documents following the death of his father-in-law. This confirmed that Henry was still at Danebridge Mill.

David Brindley, the youngest son of Henry and Betty, was baptised in 1779. He lived long enough to appear on the 1851 census for Gawsworth and confirmed that he was born in Wincle, but did that mean at Danebridge or over the river on the Cheshire side? It is not clear when Henry Brindley decided to give up milling, but by 1780 he had been associated with Danebridge Mill for nearly forty years. A succession of tenants occupied the mill well into the 19th-century, while Henry became a farmer close to Betty's family on the Gawsworth side of the boundary with Bosley and Sutton.

Henry, at Rough Hey farm, Gawsworth, lived for more than 80 years and was buried in Bosley in 1810. Probate on his estate was delayed until 1817 when its value was under £200; very much less than his brothers James, Joseph and John had accumulated from their respective businesses. Betty remained in Gawsworth until her death at the age of 93, a fact helpfully noted in the Bosley register. She had been baptised there in 1733, the surviving baby of twins born to Samuel and Mary Shaw. Betty's will named *'all my dear children'* in 1820, the year before the death of her eldest surviving son, Henry. The combined information from the wills of parents and sons reveals that Henry, her eldest son, farmed and lived for a time at Gawsworth and later at Sutton. Samuel, the second son, eventually became the miller at Mill Street, Leek, and the family were involved with premises at Mill Street and Danebridge, as well as being Cheshire farmers. Joseph also moved between Sutton and Rough Hey Farm, while David, the youngest of the brothers, farmed in Bosley and then at Hulme Walfield. Henry and Betty Brindley Snr also had three married daughters, namely, Elizabeth/Betty Lomas, Ann Hulme and Susanna Slack. Their mother died in 1827, her will bearing the label *'Mrs Brindley'*, a sign that she was respected in the community.

Henry Brindley, then of Bosley and the eldest son of Henry and Betty, married Sarah Beaman of Wincle on 9 September 1787 at Prestbury, but Sarah was buried from Sutton, at Bosley, on 3 December 1807. A James Brindley of Sutton was buried at Bosley 12 January 1809 and may have been their son, or a son of Henry and Betty, dying before his parents. Henry junior married Hannah in 1808 and had several children. Hannah died in 1820 at the age of 42 years and Henry was buried in 1821, aged 56. Both were buried in Bosley, leaving their orphaned children in the guardianship of their uncles, Samuel Brindley, Joseph Brindley, David Brindley and Samuel Shaw. The children had been baptised at Bosley and given the family names - Elizabeth, Susanna, Ann, Henry and Samuel. They were aged between four and eleven.

The farm at Sutton was modest, but better than many rural or town dwellings. Unusually at this period, an inventory was taken for probate purposes and a summary is included here as it is the only inventory of a Brindley household to come to light. Henry had a dozen or so cattle of various ages and an old mare for transport. There were essential items of farming equipment such as a cart, a plough, a harrow, ladders and a hay knife. The kitchen had a boiler, a grate and the dairying equipment - the cheese press and tub, a churn, a milk-can and milking stools. For food preservation, there was a salting stone in the buttery. Meat was placed onto the stone as on a table and rubbed with salt to keep it through the winter. The house place, or living-room, had cupboards, drawers, two tables and four old chairs, a screen, a salt and knife boxes. There was a grate, the fire irons, iron pots and an oven, which would have been built into the chimney wall. Other furnishings were a clock, a weather glass, a mirror described as a broken glass, a spring watch, a warming pan and a bookcase. The latter was worth eight shillings, but books were not mentioned. The bedrooms were simply furnished with three pairs of bed-steads, an old feather bed, a chaff bed and bolsters, the blankets, sheets and curtains. There was storage space for an old chest, a meal coffer, corn sacks and a cheese plank on which cheeses could be stored and carried. The spinning wheel was stored there too. Most of the domestic items were worth shillings and pence, while the cattle were valued at less than ten pounds each and the old mare at £5. The total was just over £87. Following the death of his father, Henry had sold his share of Danebridge Mill to his younger brothers, Joseph and David, for not more than £400.

The probate documents confirmed the names and whereabouts of Henry's brothers and all signed. Samuel Brindley was listed as the tenant of Danebridge Mill in the Land Tax Return of 1796/7, but had moved to be the miller at the mill in Mill Street, Leek, before his brother's death in 1821. Samuel had moved around Cheshire mills while his brother had tenants in Danebridge mill. A census shows that his son, another James, was born in Dane-in-Shaw, where there was a substantial corn-mill, but the child was taken to Brereton for baptism in November 1795. The register gives the child's mother as Elizabeth and she was probably the mother of Elizabeth and Henry also. The daughter Elizabeth married John Hill, while James and Henry grew up to be millers. Samuel's draft will, written in 1829, but not proven, gave his wife's name as Martha and his sons were instructed to sell the cattle and the contents of Leek mill to provide for her.

James and Henry were millers when they married and it was James who had received a clothes chest by the will of Betty, his aged grandmother. He married Ann Malkin, a great grand-daughter of Joseph Brindley of Alton. The couple settled at Ashenhurst Mill, near Lowe Hill Farm, and had two sons. Following Ann's early death, James moved into the Leek mill with a second wife, also named Ann, and brought up a large family of children. His eldest son was James Brindley, miller.

Joseph, the third son of Henry and Betty Brindley, continued to farm at Rough Hey, Gawsworth. His very long will mentioned his right and title to the Danebridge Factory in Heaton, cottages and houses in Mill Street and Clark's Bank, along with Nab Hill Cottage with its Croft (field) and garden in Leek. Joseph also had rents and ground rents from houses and buildings in Sugar Street, Macclesfield. He had invested in Sutton Lane End Sunday School and the Congleton to Buxton Turnpike, or toll road. It is possible that he was asked to survey the road by his fellow Trustees. In the previous century responsible persons in the community took the task in turn. However, Joseph called himself a 'surveyor' on the 1841 census and may have done more than report on the road. In the year that the brothers tried to sort out a worrying financial situation at Danebridge mill, Joseph made his will, but did not die until 1848.

In 1856, David Brindley, the youngest son, left an annuity to his widow from his property *'in Heaton'* Staffordshire. Presumably, this referred to the Danebridge Factory.

Before 1783, the Perkins family rented Danebridge Mill, but in the following year it was let to John Routh for cotton spinning. It is likely that he was the Quaker John Routh who was visited by Deborah Darby in 1785. She and Friend Susannah *'spent an agreeable evening with John Routh and his sister Sarah Taylor.'* Deborah Darby also visited the widowed daughter of the late Joshua Toft at Haregate Leek from time to time. On 7 June 1778, a marriage by licence had taken place at Leek between Samuel Routh of Manchester and Sarah Bradbury of Leek. Josh. Lancelot, a ribbon weaver and merchant, was a witness at the ceremony. According to Smiles, Launcelot/Lancelot was a friend of James Brindley, the engineer, and had lent him money. The relationship is unknown, but another Lancelot had married a Brindley bride in 1717. Samuel Routh was a grandson of Samuel Lucas and Margaret (nee Brindley), who had converted to Quakerism and written at length of her faith and details of life with a Brindley aunt and uncle in Leek. Margaret had been brought up in London, but married Samuel Lucas, a Quaker button merchant closely linked by business and family with James Brindley's Bowman relations.

A long lease was available for John Routh, but he only stayed for three years and Danebridge Mill was advertised in 1791 as *'a newly erected water mill or factory, four storeys high'*, with a *'very considerable number of carding and other machines'*. There was a warehouse, a store, a smith's shop, a joiner's shop, two dwelling houses and two acres of land to be let for a *'very low rent of £70'*.

A succession of tenants stayed for a year or two each

Danebridge Mill was situated just beyond this property

until a Mr Simister came in 1809. Even he sub-let the extended mill. It was advertised again in 1841. The census names families of workers in Danebridge.

In 1843, the mill was at a standstill and the deceased Henry's family had to take legal advice. There was the unpaid rent, the sub-lease and mortgage to sort out. The Brindleys, the brothers Joseph and David, wished to maintain ownership, but did not want to be liable for the mortgage arrangements of a deceased tenant. The outcome was satisfactory for the Brindleys, but they were annoyed at the state of the deserted premises. Plans for the restoration of the mill were costly and its future was in jeopardy. It survived the crisis, but was used in succession for spinning silk waste briefly, carpet printing and the manufacture of black dye. Leek became a centre for black dyeing during Queen Victoria's long period of mourning. Danebridge Mill followed this with the manufacture of black stove polish for the cast-iron stoves and fireplaces of the late Victorian and Edwardian period. Finally the site was used by a blacksmith and a wheelwright before being abandoned, ruined and then demolished in 1979 (Tony Bonson 2002).

Mills were very important in the distant past as they were the power source of small communities. Over 6,000 mills were recorded in the Domesday survey of 1086. In time, the lords of the manor took over the mills, insisting that villagers used the services of the local miller to grind their small harvest. They paid a fee to the lord, while the miller, as part of the system, became unpopular and distrusted through no fault of his own. These times passed and it is not known when the Brindley family became millers, or whether it was their hereditary occupation. However, there were Brindleys at Leek Mill before 1571 and at other watermills from time to time through the following 300 years. By then engines were required for purpose-built factories in the period now called the Industrial Revolution. James Brindley and his brothers lived in the early days of such advancement.

Nearly ten years after Brindley's death, Matthew Boulton wrote, *'The people in London, Manchester and Birmingham are all steam mill mad.'*

View from Wincle churchyard

POSTSCRIPT

The Industrial Revolution did not occur in isolation; gradual changes took place in agriculture and in the lifestyles of people. Eventually, some left the district of their roots and moved to towns which were unprepared for such numbers, creating problems in housing and sanitation. A minority were able to enjoy an improved standard of education and stood a greater chance of entering social circles far removed from those of their ancestors. Even before changes came to industry and transport, some successful craftsmen, tradesmen and farmers managed to buy a few fields, lived in improved houses with increasing levels of comfort and were, perhaps, able to educate at least one son. In this way, related families often became far apart in a few generations.

Brindley would have been unaware of remote connections such as collateral descendants of 16th century ancestors, but some attained positions worth noting here for they also made valuable contributions to the community and the advancement of knowledge in the wider field. Kinsfolk of James Brindley's grandmother Ellen Brindley illustrate the social range of even Brindley's family, described as *'humble'* on his memorial stone. Ellen Brindley's father, Henry Bowman, was the son of John and Anne Bowman, the latter being from the Beresford/Berisford family, who were long settled in the vicinity of Beresford Dale, a pretty section of the Dove valley. Mr CE Tongue, an archivist of Northampton, has established that Anne's brother, Henry Beresford (d.1660), a gentleman of Parwich, was an ancestor of the famous artist, Joseph Wright of Derby. The son of a Derby attorney, Joseph Wright (1734-1795) has significance here as he associated with men of the Midlands who discussed new inventions, new ideas and intellectual interests. At different periods of his life Josiah Wedgwood knew both Brindley and Wright. He visited Wright in Derby to purchase his fine work and would have been most surprised to have known that the two men had an ancestor in common.

Joseph Wright ARA, born in Irongate, Derby, painted dramatic landscapes of his native county as well as classical buildings, ruins and natural events such as an eruption of Vesuvius viewed on a tour of Europe. He became known as 'The Painter of Light', for his talent lay in showing a soft light on young and old faces rapt in wonder at early scientific experiments, the complexity of the working model of the solar system called an orrery, or men in the workshops of industry. A large picture, 'A Philosopher giving a Lecture upon the Orrery', hangs in Derby Art Gallery, while 'An Experiment with an Air Pump' is in the National Gallery, London. In 1992, the Tate Gallery purchased 'An Iron Forge' from Lord Romsey for £3.2m. Most artists earned a living by painting portraits and Wright's commissions came from the industrialists and gentry of the Midlands. His picture of Mr and Mrs Cotman was bought by the National Gallery for £1.3m.

Wedgwood discussed composition with Wright and bought the portrait of Dr Erasmus Darwin and two pictures, 'The Maid of Corinth' and 'The Taking of Gibraltar', the latter being considered 'sublime' by Darwin. Empress Catherine of Russia bought a dinner service from Wedgwood and three of Wright's pictures.

Wedgwood wrote that Wright would *'starve as a painter if the Empress of Russia had not some taste & sense to buy these pictures now, which we may wish the next century to purchase again at treble the price she now pays for them'*. In 1990, the Tate Gallery assembled 130 paintings, 20 drawings and 25 prints by Wright from collections in London, Paris, Prague, Moscow, St Petersburg, New York, Canada, Derby and private persons. Later the exhibition was taken to Paris and New York, but a permanent collection hangs in Derby Art Gallery.

Ellen Brindley (née Bowman) would have known her relatives in and around the small town of Leek. She must have accompanied her mother and sisters to the flourishing mercer's shop of Uncle Matthew Stubbs (c1620-1692), but as plainly clad Quakers, they were required to resist the yards of silver lace and decorative edgings. The store's extensive stock of fabrics was both practical and fashionable. There was also a piece of leather, a 'basil skin', which had been prepared for book binding. Matthew had a weaving loom and sometimes kept goats for their mohair. Matthew, possibly Alice Bowman's favourite brother, compiled an inventory of her possessions soon after her death and also that of their cousin, the Rev Josiah Stubbs (1627-1682), the Rector of Kingsley. He had a large, well-furnished rectory, with servants' quarters and a dairy, while his cattle and horses grazed on the attached land. In 1682, the Rector's collection of valuable books was worth over £100. Josiah Stubbs had attended Trinity College, Cambridge, and received an MA. In 1657 the service for his induction as the Rector of Kingsley took place during the time of Cromwell's Commonwealth and the parish register confirms that there were no disturbances. An interesting coincidence was that the Rector must have conducted the marriage service for the great-grandparents of John Gilbert. Josiah's only son Henry was briefly a curate at Cheadle, Staffordshire, but he and his young wife died soon after his father, bringing the line of descent to an end.

Ruth Stubbs (1661-1695), was Ellen Brindley's cousin and heiress to the Stubbs's properties in Butterton and elsewhere. The same age as Ellen, Ruth chose to live with her mother's relatives in Nottingham, where she occupied well-furnished accommodation. Her bedroom and sitting room held many chairs and a few luxuries, such as books, teapots, a coffee pot, silk cushions, a watch and some coal for the fire-grate. She had a side-saddle and pillion for riding. Legacies for her many relatives included Ellen, whom she described as the *'now wife'* of Joseph Brindley, meaning his then wife. Ruth Stubbs died in Nottingham and was buried at St Mary's Church on Christmas Day 1695, but she had remembered the young people of her native Staffordshire villages in her will. Seemingly ahead of her time, she established a charity for the education of an equal number of poor boys and girls in Butterton and Grindon, for 'English learning and Christian education', when few considered the education of poor girls. Ruth provided ten pounds a year for a Protestant minister in Butterton, to be essentially sound in doctrine, sober, godly and a diligent preacher. Ruth's Charity was recorded on a board hung in Butterton Church 80 years after her death and, as a respected unmarried woman, she was given the honorary title of 'Mrs'.

Ellen Brindley's aunt, Margaret Stubbs, married into the Salt family of Butterton, while Aunt Ellen married the Quaker Simon Buxton. He suffered greatly for his faith and principles, with imprisonment and many beatings for refusing to pay tithes and holding meetings, sometimes at his one time home of Coal Pit Ford, near Leek. In 1718 one of Simon's three sons, Ellen's cousin Jonathan, married into the Hammersley family of Cheddleton where George Fox, the founder of the Quaker movement, had been a noted guest in the previous century.

There was also Aunt Ann Roe (d.1698), the wife of John Roe, a yeoman of Parwich, Derbyshire, where the Roe family enjoyed tenants' rights at Roystone Grange, in nearby Ballidon. The grange is a remote farm approached by a dry valley beyond the now deserted village. Since 1979, Roystone Grange has been the subject of archaeological research, the farmer having unearthed part of a skeleton when extending his dairy. The subsequent interest in the floor of a Roman farmstead and the rooms of a medieval monastic farm has created an extension to the High Peak Trail. The Roman floor has been recovered by the Peak National Park to preserve it.

The Roes purchased land early in the 17th century and held both tenancies and freehold land. Some descendants continued farming, but one branch settled in Bakewell and produced notable parish clerks, their service receiving comment in the *Gentleman's Magazine* (Feb 1794), in books of Derbyshire interest and in their gravestone epitaphs and memorial plaques at Bakewell Church. Thomas Roe, the third son of George Roe of Ballidon, ran a successful business in ironmongery, perhaps at Roystone Grange and with further stores in Winster. The ample stocks of metal goods, foodstuffs, haberdashery and all manner of useful items had reached the small community in the hills. The Bowmans and James Brindley senior were a few miles distant, but there is no sign that they associated closely with the Roes and by 1717 Thomas Roe, the ironmonger, had died prematurely and unmarried.

Roystone Grange, Derbyshire

The ironmonger's eldest brother was a 'gentleman' with a large family, but able to educate two sons for the Church. The Rev Thomas Roe (1731-1803) bachelor, matriculated at St Edmund's Hall, Oxford, in 1751 and spent the whole of his forty-nine year ministry as curate and then vicar of Bradbourne, which included Roystone Grange. The Rev George Roe (1736-1816), his brother, had a large family and held curacies in Carsington, Ashbourne and Hayfield before returning to Parwich and, finally, the appointment as Rector of Fenny Bentley. The Rev Thomas Roe had a housekeeper and books. His brother, the Rev George, left almost £4000, school books, sermons and papers, and also dogs and 'the implements for Sporting'. His widow, née Mary Bennett, had property in Macclesfield. The clerical brothers were buried in Parwich Churchyard, where a group of Roes lie under a horse chestnut tree.

Thomas, the eldest son of the Rev George Roe, became a rector in Sotby and then Kirkby-on-Bain, in Lincolnshire. He moved in very different circles and married the sister of a Major General. She was also a daughter of an Admiral, Commander of the Fleet of Catherine the Great at the Battle of Tchesme. The two sons of Thomas attended university and his daughter, Georgiana Roe, became the daughter-in-law of the Lord Chief Justice, Thomas Denman of Dovedale, who had defended Queen Caroline in the unusual case when George IV accused his wife of adultery. Lord Denman's relative, Joseph Denman, had witnessed the will of Richard Roe of Bakewell in the previous century. The childless Georgiana became Lady Georgiana in 1854, when her Eton educated husband succeeded to the title as second baron, but a writer, JB Firth, considered that he, though accomplished and amiable, was a little eccentric as he kept black pigs and took them in his carriage as gifts for friends. Lady Georgiana died at Stoney Middleton Hall, Derbyshire, in 1871. Her husband's sister married into a family connected through marriage to a daughter of the Archbishop of Canterbury, Dr William Howley.

Ellen Brindley's brothers and sisters remained faithful to their Quaker upbringing, while the unity of the family within a network of Friends provided a degree of support no matter how geographically dispersed they had become. Henry Bowman, the eldest brother, moved from Leek in 1692 to farm Smerrill Grange, Youlgreave, where he founded a dynasty and increased his wealth considerably. Henry maintained a household with goods valued at £20, but he developed the farm to carry sheep numbering about 1000 and assessed at over £353 of his total moveable estate of £1166; a very comfortable sum in 1714. He had £400 worth of wool in store, probably 125 cwts, and cattle grazed at Smerrill Grange and on Harthill Moor. Henry's three mares provided essential transport from the isolated farm, where medieval monks had developed fish ponds in the gorge below the ancient grange. It was here that James Brindley's father may have worked for some years before his marriage, but Uncle Henry Bowman's body was returned to his Staffordshire roots when he was buried in his own Quaker burial ground in Alstonefield, in July 1714.

A great-grandson, also named Henry Bowman, became the agent, or steward, to the Earl of Bradford of Weston Park, Staffordshire, and lived in Knockin Hall, on the Earl's Shropshire estate, serving as Churchwarden at Knockin (1787-88). As Henry and his wife were childless, he left property to his unmarried sister, Hannah

Bowman, who brought water into Youlgreave, where a large stone tank has stood in the main street since 1829.

Another Henry Bowman of Smerrill Grange was a mercer, but in 1756, he married Susannah Eddowes at Prestbury Church, Cheshire. She was a daughter of a Macclesfield grocer and tobacconist, whose family bought goods from Coalbrookdale earlier in the century. Descendants of the couple married Eddowes relatives for several generations and were associated with Nantwich, Wrexham, Shrewsbury and Manchester, firstly being involved with the Eddowes's business in Macclesfield and then banking. The first Eddowes Bowman and his wife, a daughter of the Earl of Shrewsbury's editor of the *Salopian Journal*, Joshua Eddowes, had a son who lived to a great age and produced four eminent sons.

The eldest, a bachelor, lectured at the Manchester College, once known as the Warrington Academy, with which Thomas Bentley and Dr J Aikin had been associated in the previous century. He, Eddowes Bowman, was a colleague of the Rev William Gaskell, the Unitarian husband of Mrs Elizabeth Gaskell, the author of *Cranford* and the biographer of Charlotte Bronte. Mrs Gaskell, a distant connection of the Wedgwoods, knew Charles Dickens, who requested a literary contribution for his *Home Words* magazine. She wrote a story incorporating a fictitious Mr Arrowman, said to be based on a Derbyshire Bowman.

The second son of the four, another Henry Bowman (1814-1883), was an architect in Manchester, while the third son became Sir William Bowman FRS (1816-1892). The latter was a pupil at Hazelwood, in Edgbaston, a notable school founded by the Unitarian family of its headmaster Rowland Hill, later famed in postal history. William Bowman's contribution to medical knowledge was extensive and his pioneering work brought him a baronetcy in 1884. At King's College Hospital, London, his research involved the structure of striated muscle, the liver and the kidneys, parts being named after him following his discovery of how waste products are removed from the blood. William Bowman, as he was then, researched the structure of the eye at the forerunner of Moorfields Eye Hospital, advancing understanding of the organ and performing eye surgery. In 1880 Sir William was the first president of the Ophthalmological Society of the United Kingdom, being one of the first to use the ophthalmoscope.

The youngest of the four Bowman brothers was named after their father, John Eddowes Bowman, and was set for a distinguished career as Professor of Practical Chemistry in the University of London, but he died in 1856, aged 36. He and Sir William had married sisters.

The four distinguished brothers and their father are noted in the *Dictionary of National Biography* and an account of the life of Sir William Bowman appears in the *Encyclopaedia Britannica* (1987) with his photographic portrait. More than likely, these eminent men were unaware of the line of ancestry that they had in common with James Brindley, engineer.

Ellen Brindley's youngest brother, Cornelius Bowman (1666-1741), settled at One Ash Grange, near Monyash. The farm of 700 acres was an ancient place where Bowmans were to be tenants of the Dukes of Devonshire of Chatsworth House for

300 years. Situated high above beautiful Lathkill Dale, the medieval monastic sheep farm had been a place of punishment for disobedient monks from Roche Abbey, near Sheffield. Cornelius Bowman registered his house as a Quaker Meeting place and goods were taken from his family for their refusal to pay tithes, the tithes collector at one time being George Birds, no doubt a relative of the late Ruth Stubbs, on her mother's side. Bowmans travelled to the London Quaker Meeting when required and in 1754 Cornelius junior, a cousin of James Brindley senior sailed to Pennsylvania, where he visited Quakers from Derbyshire. Fourteen settlers signed the certificate for his return to Leek, declaring that he had conducted himself well.

The eldest son of Cornelius senior was another Henry Bowman, who farmed One Ash Grange on a large scale, even before his father's death. He had ample stocks of hay and corn, but his store of vast quantities of cheese must have supplied a market. Like his cousin at Smerrill Grange, Henry had invested in a large number of animals - cattle, sheep, goats, pigs and horses - over 800 of them, worth £474 of his £683 moveable estate. A cousin of James Brindley senior he died in 1748.

Each generation at One Ash Grange had a large family. Another Henry, son of the fourth Bowman tenant, Ebenezer, was involved in administration at Ackworth School, the well known Quaker foundation in Yorkshire. The distinguished statesman John Bright (1811-1889) was a pupil for one year and knew the Bowmans. John Bright was a descendant of John Gratton of Monyash, a 17th century Quaker preacher and a friend of George Fox. It has been said that John Bright spent a honeymoon with the Bowmans and, consequently, named his new house in Rochdale 'One Ash'. Bright's published diary recalled, *'We gave it the name of 'One Ash', partly in sympathy with or remembrance of the house of my ancestor, John Gratton, who lived at Monyash, near Bakewell, in Derbyshire'.* The edited diary did not mention the Bowmans. John Bright was MP for Birmingham, a noted orator and a campaigner for the repeal of the Corn Laws. Associated with many reforms, he became Chancellor of the Duchy of Lancaster in Mr Gladstone's Cabinet. One Ash Grange is still part of the Duke of Devonshire's estate and provides basic camping facilities in the barn as part of the Peak National Park's scheme for tourists.

Ellen Brindley's brother, Richard Bowman (1658-1727), who was put in charge of his sister's inheritance by his mother, was resident at Stockley Park, Tutbury, possibly with the Brindleys, for he and Elizabeth Bentley were married at Tutbury Church in 1696, the year following the baptism of the Brindley's youngest daughter at the same church. There had been a recent regulation to include Quakers in the parish records and Richard was described therein as having married *'one of his holy sisters'*. Richard's mother, Alice Bowman, had provided him with the copyhold of a farm called Clay Lake, near Leek, and he had some *'Ingagement'* with Thomas Hammersley of Old Basford, at Cheddleton. Their wives were both born 'Bentley' and may have been sisters. The childless Richard and Elizabeth moved back to Old Basford from Tutbury and Richard's will made arrangements for his youngest sister, Alice Stevenson, to do likewise, joining his widow and inheriting some basic household goods. Although the Bowmans' burial ground was at Alstonefield and the Hammersleys had a burial ground at Old Basford, Richard Bowman was buried by Quakers in Macclesfield. A Hammersley child remained close to Richard's widow and she left him a bed and a small silver spoon he regarded as his own.

The Stevensons, Joseph (d.1728/9) and Alice (1671-1742), maintained a thriving agricultural establishment at Stockley Park when many villagers had a cow, a pig and a few sheep, but Joseph Stevenson, like his Bowman brothers-in-law, had goods and animals worth a considerable sum, with a modest collection of household goods. Joseph's total estate was estimated to be over £954, Stockley Park having husbandryware valued at £42 and livestock, including a herd of ninety cattle, assessed at £600. The Stevensons must have specialised in horse breeding, as thirty-two horses and their gearings, or harness, accounted for £234. Ample foodstuffs in the form of peas, malt and the grains, corn, oats and barley, were stored. The Bowmans had arrived at Stockley Park in 1687 and the tenancy continued with the Stevensons until about 1730, the Joseph Stevensons, senior and junior, having died. Joseph senior died at the home of his mother, Ruth, in Chebsey, where there was a small community of Quakers. At Stockley Park, Alice Stevenson was the nearest, geographically, to her sister Ellen Brindley and two of Ellen's three daughters. Hannah Linnis and her family lived across the nearby fields, in Anslow, Rolleston. Prudence was at home with their mother, at least until 1729.

Ellen's sister, Ann (b.1669), died before 1711 and had been married to Joseph Davison (d.1747), the Quaker schoolmaster in Leek. He had accepted the teaching post when the offered salary was raised to £15 a year, the sum being realised with helpful contributions from other Meetings. As a Quaker, Joseph would not have been granted a teacher's licence, but suffered imprisonment for teaching without the requirement. Once, he was released by a writ from the Sheriff as he had been detained on a false charge and, on other occasions, his refusal to pay tithes resulted in the confiscation of pewter plates. Nevertheless, the Quaker school continued, Joseph's contract was renewed and he was in charge of a small library of Quaker books. Joseph also examined erring Quakers, sometimes with his sister-in-law, Alice Stevenson, following her return to the Leek Meeting.

The surviving son from Joseph Davison's marriage to Ann Bowman was Joseph jnr, father and son being involved in trade carrying a stock of fabrics worth a few hundred pounds. The son died before his father and the premises were occupied by the son of the father's second marriage, a ribbon weaver. Joseph Davison's second wife, Ruth, was the sister of Joshua and John Toft of Haregate Hall, friends of Abraham Darby II and other Quakers. Joseph's third wife was Elizabeth Beard.

At this point Quaker family connections become more complex as Ellen Brindley's sister, Esther, married into a Warwickshire family whose links complete a circle of people who were prominent in their time. Esther Bowman (1665-1734) had been left the goodly sum of £110 by her mother Alice Bowman, but it did not bring a husband from their immediate Quaker circle. Esther was 40 years old before she married 25 year old Samuel Bradford, a yeoman of Wigginshill, Sutton Coldfield, Warwickshire, and the couple did not provide the Brindleys with cousins. Samuel's stepmother was younger than Esther and he had two young half-brothers and a half-sister - Henry, John and Hannah Bradford. James Brindley's aunt, Esther Brindley, joined the household of her aunt Esther Bradford and was resident at Wigginshill when she married Quaker John Ludford there in 1714. The Ludfords lived at Baddesley Ensor, about six miles distant, but Ellen Brindley's sister, Esther Bradford, seemed fond of young Esther Ludford and Esther's daughter of the same name, leaving the latter her personal goods from the well equipped Wigginshill farm, where a Quaker burial ground and Meeting had been established. Esther Bradford's marriage settlement allowed her to retain her Bowman legacy and possessions, so that she was able to lend £100 to 'cousin' Isaac Whitehead and leave bequests to her surviving sisters when the money was returned. The first wife of Joshua Toft was a Whitehead from Wedgnock Park, Hatton, in Warwickshire. Ellen Brindley died shortly before Esther Bradford and was unable to benefit from the interest left to her by her sister. The legacy did not pass to her son, James Brindley senior.

Samuel Bradford farmed Wigginshill successfully, while his father Francis and the young family moved to Kingsbury, but Ellen Brindley's sister knew the three young people who retained their Quaker faith and became part of a tangle of relationships within the Society. Young Hannah Bradford married Allen England, a 'meat man', from Aldermills, Tamworth, while a later Allen England managed the Coalbrookdale Company's works at Bridgnorth, Shropshire (Labouchere, 1988). Moses Morris, son of a Rugeley surgeon, married Alice England and became the father of Mrs Mary Knowles, the attractive and intelligent Quakeress much admired by Dr Samuel Johnson and referred to in Boswell's famous biography of the lexicographer. Mrs Knowles and her wealthy husband were received in the Courts of Europe and she embroidered pictures of the royal princes at the request of Queen Charlotte.

The Square, Birmingham (now Old Square).

The sister of Moses Morris married William Birkbeck of Settle, Yorkshire, at a Meeting in Stafford, in 1730, and their son, Morris Birkbeck, was to marry Hannah Bradford, a daughter of John, the younger half brother of James Brindley's great-uncle Samuel Bradford. William Birkbeck's second marriage produced their descendant Dr George Birkbeck (1776-1841), whose belief in adult education led to the foundation of the Mechanics' Institute system through the country and after whom Birkbeck College, in the University of London, is named.

Henry Bradford (1689-1771), of Birmingham, was the elder half-brother of Samuel Bradford, Ellen Brindley's brother-in-law. Henry, born at Wigginshill, and his wife Elizabeth from Kendal, both Quaker ministers, settled in the new and fashionable Square (now Old Square) in central Birmingham, from the mid-1720s. At No 10, in the north east corner, they were amongst the earliest residents and conveniently situated in the vicinity of fellow Quakers and their Meeting House. Sampson Lloyd, the Quaker ironmaster, attended the same Quaker Meeting as the Bradfords, their families signing documents of the Society. Sampson Lloyd junior, founder of the well-known bank, became a Trustee of Henry Bradford's will and was described as *'my friend'*. Henry Bradford assisted Quaker Mary Farmer to become the wife of Samuel Galton, whose descendants included Sir Francis Galton (1822-1911), a cousin of Charles Darwin and a pioneer in meteorology, eugenics, colour blindness and finger printing. Eventually, the Birmingham canal system acquired a 'Farmer's Bridge' and a 'Galton Bridge'.

The Bradfords also knew the family of Jonathan Freeth, the Quaker maltster of Birmingham, to whom the first Abraham Darby had been apprenticed. Darby's use of coke in the process of iron smelting slowly revolutionised the industry, but he died in 1717 and it was Abraham Darby II, who was visited by Henry Bradford and Henry junior during the 1750s. As mentioned in Chapter 3, Henry Bradford and his son used to visit the Darbys on Quaker matters and it seems likely that Henry junior made the 1758 survey for the Birmingham and Fazeley Canal, especially as it passed close to Wigginshill, Kingsbury and Tamworth, places he knew well. Henry Bradford senior had another son, Samuel (d.1752?), a surveyor and mapmaker of some standing, whose work was engraved by Thomas Jeffreys, the King's Geographer. Between 1748 and 1752, Samuel produced excellent plans of Coventry and Birmingham, the former being preserved at the Public Record Office, Kew, while his large view of Birmingham across the fields below his father's garden at Camp Hill is hanging in a room of the Birmingham Central Library. Samuel's plan of the nearby Ravenhurst estate includes Henry Bradford's house, garden, fishpond, timberyard and sawyers' gig pit. Henry, a timberman, had left the Square and taken up residence at the Warner's Fields estate inherited from his mother's family of Fentham, who had been tanners. A later occupant of Henry's former house in the Square was John Meredith, the first solicitor of the Birmingham Canal Navigation.

Henry Bradford, a kind and generous man with a sense of humour, was interested in Quaker education and was responsible for the 'way' alongside his land becoming 'Bradford Street' and being transformed into a hive of industry. Henry offered free portions of the green fields to anyone who would build on them and carry on *'a considerable trade there'*, but the land was offered later at $^3/_4$d per square yard. By the next century Bradford Street had become a busy thoroughfare, with manufacturers of metal goods from bedsteads to wire, and a variety of items from snuff to artificial eyes.

Henry Bradford was buried at Wigginshill with his family, including Brindley's great-uncle and great-aunt, Samuel and Esther. His will named his great-nephew, Morris Birkbeck, as next in line after Henry Bradford junior; eight-year-old Morris being the son of Morris senior and Hannah, who had died soon after the boy's birth. The father and stepmother of young Morris Birkbeck took him to live in Wanborough Manor, near Guildford, Surrey, where they rented the large 16th century property from the Earl of Onslow. At a later date, Mr Gladstone visited the three-storeyed manor house with its gables, numerous chimneys and a label - 'Building of Historic Interest No 261'. The Birkbecks were able to maintain life as tenants in the imposing house with extensive farmland, where they were the first in England to breed Merino sheep. A member of the Guildford Quaker Meeting, Morris Birkbeck, senior, had a great interest in books and, after his death, the collection of several thousands was taken northward to Quakers in York, via the canal system. Including many early printed Quaker publications, the volumes are now in the Brotherton Library at the University of Leeds.

In 1817 Morris Birkbeck junior (1764-1826), a widower with several children, uprooted his family for a new beginning in America. At the age of 53 years and as a tenant of 1,500 acres of land at Wanborough Manor, he had become dissatisfied that he was not entitled to a vote or say in government. In 1814, he had ventured abroad, touring France with young George Flower of the brewing family and calling on General Lafayette. Birkbeck and Flower must have delayed their departure for America until after the death of Morris Birkbeck senior, but Flower travelled in advance of the Birkbeck party. On meeting Morris Birkbeck and his daughter in The Strand, London, William Cobbett attempted to dissuade *'the very clever man'* from leaving for the wilds of America; later recalling their conversation in his well-known book, *Rural Rides.*

Birkbeck began a diary while at sea and the family sailed with five tons of possessions in a party which included two younger sons and two daughters. General Lafayette had given them letters of introduction to the former president, Thomas Jefferson, but they made straight for the then western frontier by following the River Ohio on horseback. The Birkbecks found the cost of horses and accommodation more expensive than they had expected and Morris published advice to travellers into the interior. He observed the sale of slave women and children, vaccination for smallpox and that Pittsburgh was 'the Birmingham of America' although its population totalled only five thousand. On arrival in Illinois, he purchased land a few miles from the River Wabash and built a settlement he called 'Wanborough', while George Flower founded 'Albion'. Birkbeck rode around Illinois and became the Agricultural Society's first president, but he made a name for himself in publishing pamphlets of advice to settlers, writing to newspapers and promoting the campaign against slavery. Briefly, he was a Secretary of State, as a Democrat, but the appointment was not confirmed. Morris Birkbeck knew Dale Owen, the son of socialist Robert Owen, and their Indiana settlement called Harmony. In 1826 Birkbeck and his son, Samuel Bradford Birkbeck, returned from a visit to Harmony and attempted to cross a river on horseback, but Morris drowned and his body was taken to Harmony for burial. The settlement of Wanborough soon declined and some of the Birkbeck sons left for the silver mines of Mexico.

In 1905 CW Smith wrote that *'Morris Birkbeck exerted an influence in the development of the American nation not likely to be over estimated ...he attracted to the United States, and particularly to Illinois, a large number of specially desirable English settlers ...As an anti-slavery agitator, he rendered a service equalled by few men of his time..'.*The Chicago Historical society has a silhouette of Birkbeck at his writing desk, along with other material, and he is included in the *Oxford Companion to American Literature* (JD Hart, 1956)

The Birkbecks did not have blood ties with the Brindleys, but by marriage Samuel Bradford, yeoman of Wigginshill, was the great-uncle of Morris Birkbeck, of Illinois, and of James Brindley, the canal engineer. Through the latter's great- grandparents, the Bowmans, Ruth Stubbs, founder of a local charity, five clergymen, Lady Georgiana Denman, Thomas Roe, the ironmonger, numerous yeomen, Henry Bowman, steward to the Earl of Bradford, Hannah Bowman, who supplied Youlgreave with water, Sir William Bowman, pioneer surgeon, and Joseph Wright of Derby, artist, shared an ancestral link, in one way or another, with James Brindley. Most family history incorporates those who progress up the social scale through luck, marriage, friendship or educational opportunity, while in between are those who lead more humble lives. Naturally, information of the former is more readily available and it is hoped that the previous pages do not present the reader with an unbalanced view.

Barton Aqueduct over the River Irwell

APPENDIX

1] Was James Brindley's mother connected with this Bradbury family?

In 1670 Sampson Bradbury, a carpenter of Wincle, married Susanna Rowley at Prestbury. In 1681, this Susanna Bradbury and two of her sons inherited the lease of a property in Wincle for ninety-nine years, by the will of Edward Ashton, a carpenter of Wincle, who had some land near Sutton, Cheshire. James Brindley's sisters and their brother Henry Brindley were 'of Wincle' when they married, but neither Sampson Bradbury, nor two of his sons mentioned a Susanna who might have become the mother of James Brindley. However, the inventory of John Bradbury was contested at his death (1699) and it disclosed that he was a miller in Bosley, close to Wincle, and reference was made to the inheritance of the property. James Brindley's mother was born about January 1694/5.

2] Was Joseph Brindley, James Brindley's grandfather, connected with the Mill Street family?

There were several Brindley households in Leek before 1600. In 1571, Randal/Randle Brundle/Brindley, his wife Warber [Werburgh] and their four sons, William, Lawrence, Thomas and Ellis/Elias, were at the mill and smithy. They had farm animals and articles of husbandryware, wooden, iron and brass ware, pewter goods and bedding. The mill was passed to son William Brundle, while son Lawrence was 'to have soe much of the smithye as he neadeth'. Through the next century, there were Brindleys at the Mill Street smithy, but no reference to the mill has come to light. A line of Brindleys with the names of Lawrence, Thomas and Ellis/Elias were masons in and around Leek.

In 1676, the house with the smithy, which may have been by the old mill, had a houseplace, or living room, a little parlour, a buttery, three chambers above and a cellar. The smithy contained only a pair of wool shears and two visors. The blacksmith, Lawrence Brindley, had a horse, a mare and a pack saddle, as well as farm animals - geese, hens and £22 worth of cattle. In the 1690s, John Wedgwood of Harracles had an interest in Mill Street properties, for some were in his 'inheritance'. There were men named Joseph in this Brindley family, but did Ellen Bowman marry one of them?

3] Was James Brindley's grandfather, Joseph, a younger brother of William Brindley, a Quaker of the Booths tenement at Ipstones?

William was the eldest son of Anthony Brindley of Sheen and Ipstones, whose will (1686) named his children as William, Job (deceased, father of three daughters), Joseph, Philip, John, Isaac, Mary (m John Mellor), Dorothy (m William Johnson) and Anne (m Rev Roger Panter, Rector of Grindon). [Perhaps Anthony was the grandson of William Hall of Grindon, who named William, Anthony, Ellen, Robert, Jane, Agnes and Margaret Brindley as children of his daughter and son-in-law, William Brindley (1640/1)].

Anthony Brindley of Sheen and Ipstones left the Booths tenement to his eldest son, William, in 1686 and the initials WB 1687, on a farm building at Booths Hall, were noted in The Tale of Ipstones (Rev F Brighton, 1937). Anthony's third son, Joseph, was left £30 by the same will, but was instructed to come to receive it at the end of seven years following Anthony's death. No explanation was given for the exceptionally long wait. Was this Joseph married to Ellen Bowman? Anthony's estate totalled almost £150.

William Brindley married Sarah Hammersley, both Quakers. Their only child, also named Anthony, married Elizabeth Jackson and died before his father, leaving their only child, Sarah Brindley, to inherit the Booths tenement from grandfather William in 1714. Their home had a 'house' or living room, a dining room, a garret and two chambers over the house, including 'Sarah's chamber', where she had a feather bed and a stand 'to set a candle upon'. The contents of William's fairly comfortable household and his moveable possessions were worth £37.

In 1720 Sarah married John Winter, a Quaker mercer from Stafford. He was soon bankrupt, having bought some old stock, and a financial arrangement was made with a member of the Hodgetts family of Stafford. The latter died and the arrangement passed to a Hodgetts of Shut End, Kingswinford. By 1751 the widowed Mrs Sarah Winter, who had outlived her two children, wished to sell the property. The legal tangle with the Hodgetts was taken to the Middle Temple, in London, and Sarah won her case. An abstract confirms her descent from great-grandfather Anthony and that a Joseph was her great-uncle, but was he the grandfather of the canal engineer?

In 1743 Sarah Winter had dealings with Joshua Toft, concerning a house, a barn, gardens and 156 acres. In 1756, a deed involved the Booths tenement, the Gilbert brothers, John Hammersley, William Gent, his cousin George Goodwin of Monyash and John Goodwin of Ashbourne. Brindley, the millwright, had received payments from Goodwin of Monyash for mill work. A William Gent had married a daughter of the Janney family at Booths Hall in the previous century. Could it have been mere coincidence that John Brindley, a brother of the engineer, moved into a home of a Hodgetts in Kinver, forty years later? Hodgetts had been landowners affected by the Staffordshire and Worcestershire canal development.

4] The lease of Danebridge Mill, in 1742, referred to 'the will of Mary Parker of Derby'. The Calendar of Wills in Lichfield Record Office gives the name 'Margaret Parker', as does the original wrapper of the will. The will (probate 26 April 1737) is that of 'Margery Parker' and she signed it so. Her two gentleman friends were named on the Danebridge Mill lease and in her will. She was a spinster given the title 'Mrs'. She had inherited from her father, Joseph Parker, or indirectly through her brothers. Her two brothers were deceased and so Mary Parker, her young niece, inherited goods from 'Margery'. This Mary Parker later married Mr John Fletcher of Stainsby House, Horsley, in Derbyshire. The second lease and release (1743 New Calendar) relating to Danebridge Mill named her husband and gave his address. On marriage, her property would have passed to her husband. His father, another John Fletcher, had left him several coal and iron mines in Derbyshire, Nottinghamshire and Warwickshire. Was the colliery at Bedworth one of his?

Transport Commission

MSS SOURCES

REGISTERS - SRO, CRO, DRO

Bishop'sTranscripts and Marriage Bonds - LJRO, CRO
Quaker Records - SRO, NRO
Birmingham Meeting and Friends' House Library, Euston
Wills - LJRO, SRO, CRO, PRO

CHAPTER 1

SRO D3159	Staffs and Leek Quaker records.
SRO D239/M, 3055	Egerton/Stubbs, Mortgage by Lease
WSL 206B/10/74	Beresford Papers. From a soldier's diary
WSL 206B/12/74	Alstonefield Quaker Burial Ground (copy)
WSL	Miscellaneous card index - Bowman pedigree
WSL SR230 85/45	Transcript of will of James Brindley, senior, (1773)
LJRO	6 May 1773, James Brindley, Leek. (senior), will.
	18 Dec 1772, James Brindley, Wolstanton, (Adm.)

CHAPTERS 2-6

N'land RO 2/DE/6/3/1	William Brown's letter (1759)
N'land RO 2DE/7/4/2	James Brindley's letter (1765)
N'land RO 2/DE/7/4/9	Thomas Broad's letter (Sept 1759)
N'land RO 2/DE/7/4/10	Thomas Broad's letter (Dec 1759)
SCLA SRM 14/S.815 (o/s)	Norton-in-the-Moors (Henshall, 1771)
SRO D593/H/9/1	Staffordshire Canal (later Trent & Mersey). Brindley, revised by Smeaton (1760) Plan
SRO D593/H/2-3	Plan of canals made by Brindley. Printed for the Duke of Bridgewater (1769)
SRO mf 79	S&W Canal records, especially on reels 1-8 (1766-1772)
	Reel 1 -Discharge of Brindley, 1772;
	Reel 6 - Letter from Brindley in London; Jan 1769, genuine signature of James Brind…
WSL M727/1-5	Includes Brindley's estimate for Lichfield Canal (1758-9)
WSL 196/159-60/77	Ditto.
WSL 93/23/41	Goldenhill estate (1818)
WSL 44/116/41	Goldenhill estate (1760)
WSL 44/286 a & b/41	Goldenhill estate (December 1772)
WSL SR 230 85/6/42	HH Williamson`s declaration (1840)
WSL SR 230 85/4/42	Lithograph of facsimile of Droitwich letter 7 May 1769. Original at Univ of Keele.
BCL L78.1 BRI 5000971	Photostat of Brindley`s notebook (1755-58)
BCL MS 1633/3	Wedgwood's letters to Dr E. Darwin; Apr 1765, 4 May 1765, 10 July 1765.
BCL	Boulton and Watt Papers
	Box 2/12/1 John Gilbert to Matthew Boulton 23 Apr 1779
	Letter Box 2 Reel 2: James Watt to Gilbert 29 Apr 1779
	Misc. box of drawings: B&W for John Gilbert 27 Feb 1789
	Box 4 Bundle 'G': Letter about engines and meetings 16 May 1789
	Box 4 Bundle 'G': Gilbert jnr asks for surveyor 4 Jun 1791
	Box 6 Bundle 'G': Gilbert jnr to Mr Boulton (1800)

CHAPTER 7

Keele University Library	Wedgwood Collection, 31-32021
SRO D801/2/3/7	John Brindley, PCC will (copy) 1808
SRO D801/2/3-	series concerning John Brindley & Kinver property
SRO D538/C/19/14	Letter making ref. to grant of arms (1875)
SRO D240/D/80; 92; 134; 242	Brindleys at Alton
SRO D239/M/2493	Tideswell of Oakamoor (1821)
SRO D538/2/56	Draft of Joseph Brindley's Mill Street property (1790)
SRO D538/C/19/13	Draft will of Samuel Brindley, Leek, 11 Feb 1829
SRO 4974/B/5/69	Swythamley Papers/Danebridge

POSTSCRIPT	Quaker records as named above.
	BCL and PRO Kew for Samuel Bradford's plans.

APPENDIX

SRO D239/M/752	Abstract of Mrs Sarah Winter's case.
SRO D605/1/1-24	Deeds including Brindley/Winter/Gilbert/Toft
CRO WC 1699	John Bradbury, miller, Bosley, contested inventory.